73

The Great Pyramid
Cairn

73
The Great Pyramid
Cairn

Erik Jacoby & Johanna Friesen

Cairn Publishing
73Cairn.com

© 2021 Cairn Publishing, P.O. Box 551, Garden Valley, CA 95633

ISBN #979-8-9855688-1-3 (Gray Scale Edition)

Printed and bound in U.S.A.

All Inquiries: 73Cairn.com

Menkaure
51.34°

300,000 km/second

Khafre

53.1667°

26° 34' 23"

Khufu

51.844°

Special thanks to Mathew Marx and Robert Hall, two of the smartest people I know. I really appreciate the time each of you devoted to this book and I am grateful for your invaluable advice.

To Allen Gunn: your JAVA programming class helped me see part of this solution. Thank you, Gunner!

To David DeVault, my go-to computer technologist who shared his bandwidth to assure that the bytes would travel where they were needed. Thanks, David!

And a very special thanks to Johanna Friesen. Her interest in the Bible and her ability to understand my hypothesis added a depth to this book that I probably could not have expressed without her contributions.

CONTENTS

FORWARD

How This Book Came To Be

I have been fascinated by the stars in the heavens since I was a small boy. My fascination with the Giza pyramid complex began in my youth as well. By commingling my two greatest interests, Astronomy and the Giza pyramid complex, I was able to examine the most mysterious wonder of the world through "galactic glasses."

My examination of the Giza pyramid complex and its elements began thirty years ago. During these thirty years of investigation, my hypothesis as to what their purpose is has changed several times. My ongoing investigation and analysis of evidence has culminated in the information presented in this book. I realize, and welcome the fact, that further investigation and analysis of the evidence presented in this book may lead to adjustments to my hypothesis by me, or by others.

I began my investigation of the Giza pyramid complex

by testing the validity of others' ideas about why the Giza pyramid complex was built. I had many reasons to reject the notion that the pyramids at Giza were primarily constructed as burial chambers for the pharaohs Khufu, Khafre, and Menkaure. In the chapter titled, "Why the Giza Pyramid Complex Was Built", I will present my evaluations of past hypotheses and explain how I arrived at my hypothesis on the subject.

Through my examination of the construction of the Giza Pyramids and other pyramids, I have also decided that the Giza pyramid complex may not have been constructed exclusively by normal human beings. In the chapter titled, "Who Did Build the Giza Pyramid Complex?", I present an alternative explanation to the generally accepted idea for how the Giza pyramids were constructed and who performed the construction labor.

It is my hypothesis that the Giza pyramid complex is a celestial map. I believe that this hypothesis is the key to answering what I consider to be the most important question of all: what is the contemporary purpose of the Giza pyramid complex? In the chapter titled, "The Giza Pyramid Complex Galactic Map", I will present my evidence for such and explain why I do not agree with other similar "theories" that have been presented in the past.

During my investigation of the Giza pyramid complex, I discovered the works of John Taylor and Charles Piazzi Smyth, who were friends interested in the significance of the Great Pyramid (Khufu Pyramid). John Taylor hypothesized that the Golden Ratio and Pi were intentionally incorporated into the construction of the Great Pyramid. Piazzi Smyth further hypothesized that these geometrical concepts were so advanced for the time of the construction of the Great Pyramid that its construction must have been directed by God. Since the publication of Piazzi Smyth's first book, *Our In-*

heritance in the Great Pyramid in 1874, the link between God and the construction of the Great Pyramid has not been further explored much. However, Piazzi Smyth's hypothesis did intrigue me enough to present it to my wife, whom I had engaged in the composition of *73, The Great Pyramid Cairn*, and who has much interest in God.

　　More recently, my wife and I have become better Bible students. I recognize that, in the not too distant past, scientific and religious scholars may have felt that their interpretations of evidence for historical events were not in agreement. However, my analysis of the Giza pyramid complex has resulted in a hypothesis which cannot deny either interpretation. Hence, I have used the Bible to help me synthesize the astronomical discoveries (the "what" and "where" elements of discovery that I made using the Giza pyramid complex) with answers to the "when", "who", and "why" questions my discoveries created for me. The scientific and religious evidence I discovered are presented throughout this book. In the chapters titled, "The Giza Pyramid Complex: Word of God" and "The Giza Pyramid Complex Revelation", I present my synthesis of scientific evidence with biblical understanding.

　　In *73, The Great Pyramid Cairn*, I will present you with hard evidence (photographs, diagrams, and mathematical equations) the likes of which have never been presented before and present a new hypothesis for when the Giza pyramid complex was built, who built it, and why it was built. Please join me on this astronomical and biblical journey into the past and into a future filled with promise, productivity, and peace for all.

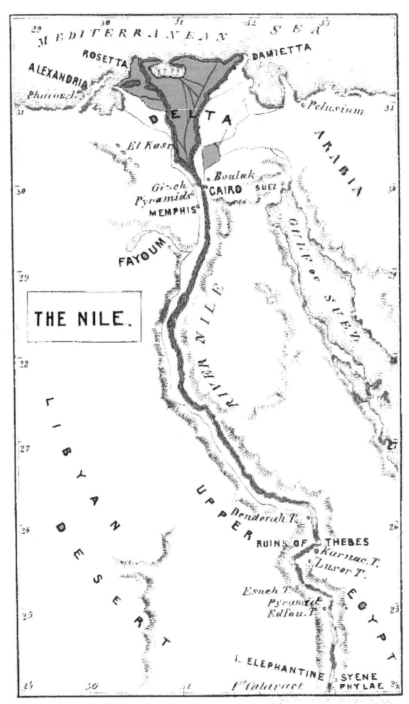

Ancient Egypt, Its Monuments and History, 1851
D. P. Kidder

Chapter 1

Studying the Giza Pyramid Complex

Over the past two hundred years, interest in the Giza pyramid complex has steadily grown. With the recent use of the internet and social media to share experiences and ideas, there has been a renaissance of curiosity about pyramids, in general, and the Great Pyramid (Khufu Pyramid) specifically. Visiting the pyramids in Egypt is on many people's bucket list and is definitely on mine. Before I can make my way to Egypt though, I am dependent on the works of study presented by Egyptologists from diverse backgrounds and disciplines whose presentation of evidence dates back decades, centuries, or millennia.

One Egyptian historian, Manetho, who is thought to have been an Egyptian priest, authored *Aegyptiaca (History of Egypt)* sometime between 323 BC and 283 BC. In *Aegyptiaca*, Manetho provides a chronology of the reigns of pharaohs beginning with Sneferu (3998 to 3969 BC). Pharaoh Sneferu was succeeded by his son, Khufu, and Manetho lists Pharaoh Khufu's reign as 3969 BC to 3908 BC. Pharaoh Khufu was succeeded by his son, Khafre who reigned from 3908 BC to 3845 BC. And Pharaoh Khafre's son and successor, Menkaure, reigned from 3845 BC to 3784 BC.

In his book *The Complete Pyramids*, Mark Lehner, an American archaeologist, lists the reigns of the same pharaohs as follows: Pharaoh Sneferu (2575 BC to 2551 BC), Pharaoh Khufu (2551 BC to 2528 BC), Pharaoh Khafre (2520 BC to 2494 BC), and Pharaoh Menkaure (2490 BC to 2472 BC). Mark Lehner based this chronology on the work of Professor John Baines, a British Egyptologist, and Dr. Jaromir Malek, both from the University of Oxford and coauthors of *Atlas of Ancient Egypt*.

Brian Fagan, Professor Emeritus of anthropology at the University of California in Santa Barbara, also credits Manetho as the priest who documented the reigns of the pharaohs. In his book *Egypt of the Pharaohs*, Dr. Fagan states that the Pyramids of Giza were constructed between 2550 BC and 2472 BC by Khufu, his son Khafre, and his grandson Menkaure.

If Manetho is accurate and Professor John Baines, Dr. Jaromir Malek, and Dr. Fagan are not, Khufu, Khafre, and Menkaure did reign as pharaohs 400 to 600 years before samples of hieroglyphs appeared. However, if Manetho's documents are not accurate, hieroglyphs appeared 650 to 850 years before the reign of Pharaoh Khufu. Regardless of the exact dates that their reigns occurred, the order in which things occurred- hieroglyphics, then the first pharaoh, is generally accepted to be true.

In all of my research, I have not been able to find a historical explanation for why or how two chronologies of the pharaohs differ by nearly 1440 years, except for one. The only possible explanation I can give for the discrepancies in dates is that the Vatican did decree that the Great Pyramids at Giza could not possibly predate the occurrence of the Great Flood in the Holy Bible. In the early 1800s, papal families devoted resources to the promotion of this decree of the Vatican by financing such endeavors as the "collection" of relics by Giovanni Belzoni and his wife, Sarah Banne, to be displayed in relic museums for the generation of capital for the Vatican Bank. In my opinion, by obtaining the Egyptian relics and displaying them in their museums, the Vatican could rewrite history to match their interpretation of God's Word, the Bible.

Please understand that, as a student of God's Word as well, I do not present this information to offend any other students of the Bible. As we all learn if we study in depth, humans are sometimes driven by one or more of the Seven Deadly Sins (pride, envy, gluttony, greed, lust, sloth, and wrath.) And, being under the influence of one or more of these Deadly Sins, their determination to alter the truth to fit their paradigm (world view) will lead them to perform behaviors not considered holy.

For example, in one biographical presentation of the discovery of the "pharaoh" Hatshepsut's mummy and tomb, we are told that she ruled Egypt from 1479 BC to 1457 BC. We are also told that, for reasons "unknown," her successor, Pharaoh Thutmose III (her husband's only surviving son by a harem girl) who reigned from 1457 BC to 1425 BC, had every mention of Hatshepsut scratched out of the records during his second decade as Pharaoh. In this presentation, we are led to believe that Pharaoh Thutmose III resented his ambitious stepmother's achievements. This was the interpretation I accepted until I came across new evidence.

In his book *Egypt of the Pharaohs*, Dr. Brian Fagan

relayed that until two-year-old Thutmose III came of age twenty-two years later, Queen Hatshepsut ruled. A concurrent court architect, Ineni, left documentation of the reigns of both Queen Hatshepsut and Pharaoh Thutmose III. Ineni characterized Hatshepsut as deceitful, manipulative, and abusive to her people. He wrote that, in her mortuary temple, which she had built during her reign, Hatshepsut had herself depicted in the regalia of a male ruler. She even had her coronation as pharaoh (an event which had never happened) depicted on the walls of her mortuary temple. This is a prime example of the lengths to which humans will go to present their truth to the world when they have the authority and the resources to do so.

According to Ineni, Thutmose III was an adept military leader, and Ineni gave him much credit for his ability to conquer yet show great diplomacy and acceptance toward the newly consolidated provinces. Egyptologists have dubbed Thutmose III the "Napoleon of Egypt" based on his legacy. With respect to the truth, now I must consider that perhaps Thutmose III scratched out his stepmother's false depictions to remove her lies from history. And, he may have waited to do so until after her death, which would have been a diplomatic move.

These are prime examples of how difficult it is to research ancient Egypt. Even when relics (discovered art, tools, and documents) are meticulously collected by archaeologists, analyzed, carefully cataloged, and publicly displayed in museums, the public is presented with a generally accepted chronology of when the relics came to be, who may have used them, and what they were used for. Then, scholars try to use documents (the writings of men) to aid with this sorting. I am certain that every honest seeker of truth involved in every one of these discoveries wants to present their findings as accurately and as scientifically as possible at the time of their discoveries. Unfortunately, as I have stated previously, we must accept the possibility that the documents they are using may not accurately depict the truth.

There is also the possibility that certain truths have been withheld by certain people in order to protect human kind, or to reserve delivery of such information for future humans. I am most inclined to believe this possibility, in conjunction with barriers to accurate science, as the two primary reasons why people still have questions about the Giza pyramid complex.

I feel it is essential that my readers understand my perspective and commitment to providing you with the best documentation available, since other famous Egyptologists are comfortable accepting that "virtually all information in archaeology is circumstantial" (as stated by Mark Lehner, Archeaologist with the Oriental Institute of the University of Chicago and Harvard Semitic Museum.) Personally, I believe that some mathematical analysis could provide us with clearer answers to our questions regarding the Giza pyramid complex.

Of all the academic disciplines, I hold math in the highest regard because fundamental mathematical concepts can be physically proven. Of all the historical documentation I have read, I hold God's Word in the highest regard because, through the millennia and despite variation in translations, later prophets reiterated earlier prophecies and those prophecies were eventually realized. In the Bible, God warns us repeatedly of the dangers of holding the government of man in higher regard than the Realm of God. Throughout history, God has annihilated entire civilizations for doing so. God's Word is the only incorruptible truth and God is the highest authority. Thus, the research in this book is my attempt to find where God's Word and mathematics intersect. I believe that the original components of the Giza pyramid complex were built for this very purpose. Hence, when I present you with my alternate hypothesis, math will be used as evidence. But, have no fear. I will help you through it all.

Because I am only a Bible student and not a theologian, I do not feel qualified to direct the reader regularly to specific Bible books, chapters, or verses. However, I hope that my references to historical events documented in the Bible, Torah, and Koran will inspire my readers to study their versions of God's Word and/or encourage them to consult their religious leaders for deeper understanding of the historical events I refer to in this book. In other words, don't take my word for it, and do your own research. That is what I did, and I invite my readers to question my authority on the subject as well.

Welcome aboard and enjoy the voyage!

Chapter 2

Pyramids, Not Built To Be Burial Chambers

I will begin my presentation of research findings by challenging the most popular hypothesis about why the Giza pyramid complex was built: that the pyramids at Giza were built with the primary purpose of being burial chambers for the pharaohs. I believe that this is not what the pyramids were built for, even though there is circumstantial evidence that they may have been used for such a purpose at some time.

By late 2002, after twelve years of detailed examination of the three pyramids at Giza and other elements in the Giza pyramid complex, I became convinced that the pyramids had not originally been built to be burial chambers for Khufu, Khafre, and Menkaure, to whom credit has been given for their construction. I am not suggesting that Khufu, Khafre, and Menkaure were not capable of directing the construction of pyramids or other elements in the Giza pyramid complex. Much energy has been devoted to proving how the pyramids could have been built by the efforts of human beings. However, I can provide evidence that the three pyramids at Giza were not constructed by Khufu, Khafre, and Menkaure to be burial chambers.

First of all, not one of the three pyramids at Giza contains even one hieroglyph. The use of hieroglyphs had already been a part of Egyptian written language by the reign of Pharaoh Khufu (2551 BC to 2528 BC, according to Mark Lehner, an American archaeologist). Pharaoh Khufu was chronologically the first of the three pharaohs who typically are accredited with the construction of the three largest pyramids in the Giza pyramid complex. Pharaoh Khufu is said to have ordered the construction of The Great Pyramid, the largest pyramid ever built. Hieroglyphs had already appeared on other structures (beginning about 3400 BC to 3200 BC) and were used to document key historical events. Hieroglyphs exist on the walls of other architectural sites, burial sites, and on sarcophagi (stone "boxes" in which pharaohs' mummy-wrapped bodies were buried within a wooden "coffin" painted with the youthful likenesses of the pharaohs). Pharaohs' entire biographies were depicted on the walls of their burial sites elsewhere. Their biographies were meticulously inscribed, and they definitely described each of the pharaohs' reigns in a most positive light.

So, why are there no hieroglyphs in the Giza pyramids?

Clearly, if the three pyramids at Giza had actually been built to be their burial chambers, they would have been filled with hieroglyphs depicting the details of the construction of these most magnificent pyramids. Certainly, the three pharaohs would have wanted their legends to be eternally inscribed in stone, as had become customary by the time of their rule. However, there is not one hieroglyphic inscription in any of the three pyramids.

Neither mummies nor remnants of mummies have ever been found in any pyramid within the Giza pyramid complex. Although there may be a plausible, yet unsavory, explanation for why mummies may have been removed from their original resting places, it is unlikely that genetic material has never been found. There is documentation that extricated mummies were a valuable commodity. Once a mummy is exposed to air, it begins to dry and will quickly disintegrate. The resulting "bitumen" was ground into a powder and sold as medicine to consumers who believed that the mummy powder had special healing powers. There is no discussion of this practice in ancient Egyptian hieroglyphics. However, beginning in the 12th Century AD, there is documentation of such commerce, which extended into Europe and Asia well into the later 1800s. Nonetheless, traces of ancient genetic material would still be within the sarcophagi, yet none has been reported to have been found.

On the other hand, we shouldn't be surprised that so many nonhuman relics may have been removed from the Giza pyramid complex (as well as from other burial sites such as the Valley of the Kings in Luxor, where no pyramids were built at all). What do exist in other burial sites, to this day, are the hieroglyphs. In the Valley of the Kings, used as a burial site from the 16th to 11th centuries BC, the stone walls and sarcophagi bear hieroglyphics memorializing the lives and reigns of each of the pharaohs buried there.

It is only because of the devoted ancient historians' efforts that today we have documentation as evidence that some of those relics ever existed. For example, in 449 BC, Herodotus, an ancient Greek historian, documented the existence of carvings of animals on polished stone blocks (reliefs) along the causeway that led to Khufu's pyramid. Herodotus described the causeway in great detail and even documented its length as one kilometer (yet, a modern Egyptologist believes it was only 825 meters long). This causeway no longer exists, so we are indebted to Herodotus for his efforts.

Other evidence of the removal of relics is sometimes revealed when the relics are discovered many miles away. For example, by five hundred years after Khufu is credited with having built the pyramid named after him at Giza, reliefs on his temple outside the pyramid had been stripped off and reused on other structures at the burial site of a later pharaoh. Archaeologists make such determinations by comparing the artistry of the relic in question to other relics identified to be of the same period.

The sarcophagus found in the Bent Pyramid in Dahshur, built by Pharaoh Sneferu, Khufu's father, was about three times the size of the stone box found in the "burial chamber" in the Giza pyramid accredited to Khufu. It was made of granite, as the one in the Khufu pyramid was. However, Sneferu's sarcophagus was ornately decorated with hieroglyphs, whereas Khufu's sarcophagus does not have a single decoration or hieroglyph. Why would the builder of the first perfectly designed pyramid at Giza have been buried in an unadorned red granite box?

Could the explanation for the lack of hieroglyphs in the burial chambers of the Pharaohs Khufu and Khafre be the result of their having been exceptionably humble leaders? The historical documents do not paint such a picture. Herodotus wrote that, under Khufu, the country had been reduced "to a completely awful condition." He relayed that gangs of 100,000 men worked for three months without a break. They were paid in radishes, onions, garlic, and bread loaves (and maybe a little beer). Herodotus even claimed that Khufu had forced his daughter to sell her favors to pay for his tomb. Herodotus wrote that Khafre, Khufu's son, was similarly unpleasant and that the Egyptians hated them both. Menkaure, however, is depicted by Herodotus as the ruler who ended the tyranny of his father and grandfather, and the sarcophagus in the pyramid accredited to Menkaure was artistically adorned, yet not with hieroglyphics.

On the other hand, many hieroglyphs and ornamentations were reported by Herodotus to be on the walls of the causeways leading from each pyramid to the mortuary temple of each corresponding pharaoh. Only the mortuary temple of Menkaure still remains, and Menkaure's mortuary temple was the largest and most ornately decorated, according to Herodotus. Thus, a positive correlation between the popularity of a pharaoh and the artistry of their temple might be made. However, I still must ask whether or not Pharaoh Khufu, Pharaoh Khafre, and Pharaoh Menkaure were ever actually buried in each of the pyramids which bear their names today.

I would argue that they were each buried elsewhere and that the assumption that they may have been buried within the pyramids exists only because it seems very likely that Pharaoh Menes, the first pharaoh, was buried in the ornately decorated sarcophagus within his pyramid. I can believe that Pharaoh Menes was buried in his sarcophagus because it had the dimensions which left ample room for a wooden coffin large enough to hold a mummy wearing a death mask, as was traditional. On the other hand, the sarcophagi in each of the Giza complex pyramids are much smaller. The red granite sarcophagus in Khufu's pyramid has the external dimensions 98.7cm x 105.1cm x 227.6cm, leaving no room for a wooden coffin. An expedition, led by R. Howard-Vyse in 1837, removed the sarcophagus they found within Menkaure's pyramid, which he determined to be made of basalt, and placed it on a ship to be brought to England. The ship with the sarcophagus sank, and only sketches, by Howard-Vyse, of Menkaure's sarcophagus survived. According to his sketches, the internal dimensions of the sarcophagus were six feet long by two feet wide by two feet high, with external dimensions of eight feet long by three feet wide and three feet high to the lid. Again, these dimensions leave only enough room for a mummy and not enough room for an ornate coffin to house the mummy. I have not been able to find the dimensions of the sarcophagus in Khafre's pyramid, which was made of black granite; however, Petrie noted that it was too large to fit through the passageway leading to the "burial chamber" and suggested that the rest of the pyramid must have been built around it. Although a coffin with a mummy could have been maneuvered to the sarcophagus, the coffin would not have fit within it. Hence, it does appear that the builders intended to make it impossible to remove the sarcophagus without damaging the pyramid. In other words, it was very important to the builders of Khafre's pyramid that the sarcophagus remain within the pyramid forever.

In 2018, a cache of mummified animals were discovered in a priest's burial tomb in Saqqara which were determined to have been mummified about 2600 years ago, based on the analysis of the cat mummies. Thirty sarcophagi were discovered in Luxor in 2019. They are believed to be about 3,000 years old. Also in 2019, several dozen more sarcophagi, deemed to be about 2,000 years old, were discovered near the Step Pyramid of Djoser in Saqqara. To date, no sarcophagus has ever been found inside of an ancient pyramid. Only small, more modern pyramids have been found to contain human remains. This suggests that the practice of burying mummies inside of, or near pyramids, was more recent than the accepted building dates of the Giza pyramid complex.

In my opinion, the evidence is clear that neither Pharaoh Khufu, nor Pharaoh Khafre, nor Pharaoh Menkaure were ever buried in their respective pyramids, nor were the respective pyramids built with such a purpose in mind. So, you might ask now, what were the pyramids built for? I am so glad you asked.

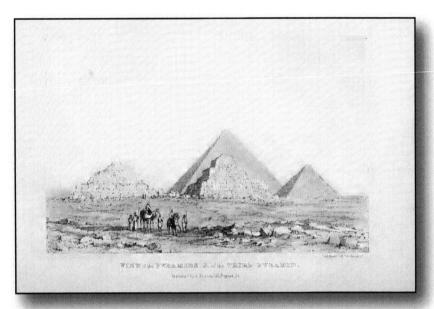

Operations Carried On At the Pyramids Of Gizeh in 1837 Vol. 1, 1840
Howard-R Vyse

The Pyramids and Temples of Gizeh, 1883
W. M. F. Petrie

Chapter 3

When Was The Giza Pyramid Complex Built?

Before I tell you why I believe the Giza pyramid complex was built, I need to discuss *when* I think it was built. More accurately, I need to explain why my hypothesis is not in agreement with the timelines for the building of the pyramids. To be precise, I believe that either the year the Giza pyramids are believed to have been built is not correct, or the order in which all pyramids were constructed is incorrect. Both timelines cannot be correct. Perhaps, neither timeline is correct.

The generally accepted timeline is that the era of pyramid building began in the 3rd dynasty, ending the Early Dynastic Period. The first pyramid was a step pyramid built by Djoser (Netjerykhet) in Saqqara (14 km southeast of Giza). Then, Sekhemkhet attempted to build a step pyramid nearby to the southwest of Djoser's and Khaba made his attempt to build a layer pyramid 8 km northwest in Zawiyet El-Aryan.

Then, in the 4th Dynasty (the beginning of the Old Kingdom), Pharaoh Sneferu built the step pyramid in Meidum (18 km south of Saqqara). When Sneferu moved with his court 10 km north to Dahshur, he constructed two more pyramids: the Bent Pyramid and the Red Pyramid to the north. Sneferu's son, Pharaoh Khufu (Cheops), then built his giant pyramid in Giza. Then, the next pyramid was built 8 km north in Abu Roash and is credited to Pharaoh Djedefre. Next, Khufu's son, Pharaoh Khafre (Chephren) returned to build his large pyramid directly to the southwest of Khufu's pyramid in Giza. And Khafre's son, Pharaoh Menkaure (Mycerinus), built his significantly smaller pyramid directly to the southwest of Khafre's pyramid. It was the last pyramid to be built in Giza.

In the 5th Dynasty, three pyramids were built in Saqqara, and three pyramids were built in Abusir (3 km north of Saqqara). In the 6th Dynasty, all four pyramids were built in Saqqara, with three of the four built in South Saqqara. In the 8th Dynasty, only one pyramid was built in South Saqqara.

In the 12th Dynasty (the Middle Kingdom), eight pyramids were built: three in Dahshur, two in Lisht (2 km north of Meidum), one in Illahun (2 km southwest of Meidum), one in Hawara (1 km west of Illahun), and one pyramid in South Mazghuna (2 km south of South Dahshur). In the 13th Dynasty, the last two pyramids were built 6 km north in South Saqqara, but the last major pyramid, built by Khendjer around 1745 BC, was left unfinished.

However, Khendjer's pyramid was not the end of pyramid building altogether. The pyramids built in the New Kingdom were smaller. Some pyramid complexes included many small "private" pyramids. These pyramid complexes were very crowded.

The architectural evolution of pyramid building had a

sudden beginning. Djoser made his attempt to build a pyramid around 2615 BC which resulted in a step pyramid (with a volume of 330,400 cubic meters) in Saqqara. The next two pyramid builders, Sekhemkhet and Khaba, were unable to complete their small pyramid projects even though they were each about one-tenth the volume of Djoser's step pyramid. Pharaoh Sneferu's first pyramid in Meidum was a step pyramid (with a volume of 638,733 cubic meters) and was nearly twice the volume of Djoser's. Pharaoh Sneferu's second pyramid, a bent pyramid, was twice the volume of his first. And the first pyramid that actually achieved a successful pyramidal design, built by Pharaoh Sneferu in Dahshur around 2550 BC, was more than two and a half times the volume of his step pyramid and thirty percent more voluminous than his bent pyramid. Then, within 20 years, Pharaoh Khufu built his pyramid in Giza to be more than 50% larger than Sneferu's (with a volume of 2,583,283 cubic meters).

It seems that, architecturally, Pharaoh Khufu's pyramid may have been as large as possible to build with the technology, tools, and manpower available in the Old Kingdom. Although Pharaoh Djdefre's unfinished pyramid in Abu Roash had a volume only five one hundredths that of Khufu's, the next pyramid, built by Pharaoh Khafre in Giza, was built to nearly the same dimensions as Khufu's pyramid. Suddenly, the size of subsequent pyramids became smaller with Pharaoh Menkaure's pyramid at Giza measuring not quite one tenth the volume of Khafre's pyramid. And most of the subsequent pyramids built thereafter were just as small with many even half the size of Menkaure's pyramid.

Upon reviewing the timeline of pyramid building and the evolution of the architectural designs of the pyramids, you might ask, as I do, how the construction and size of the pyramids evolved so quickly and deevolved just as quickly (within about 100 years). In the history of the development of any form of architecture, there have been no other deevolutionary periods to resemble this one. Typically, when an architectural design is found to be successful, it is repeated. And the most revered members of a society typically make the largest structures. So, why were only two "great" pyramids built? Was there a lack of materials or labor? A lack of food? A lack of community? What prevented the replication of "great" pyramids?

A short answer to these questions is that Egyptians' survival was, and still is, dependent on the Nile River. The Nile River swells and narrows dramatically every year, and each year can be very different from the year before or the year to come. Food had to be produced for laborers, and structures cannot be built successfully on swampy soil. Evidence still remains that some pharaohs did choose the wrong land to build on. There is documentation that there was low flood during the reign of Djoser which led to food shortages. Sneferu had trouble with sinkage while building his bent pyramid (his second attempt at pyramid building in Meidum).

In contrast, during the reigns of Pharaoh Khufu and Pharaoh Khafre, there is evidence that food was plentiful and many citizens were attracted to the Giza pyramid complex site for some purpose. A very complex hierarchical system rewarded loyalty with riches and, sometimes, a resting place within the complex.

I am troubled by the fact that Menkaure's pyramid in the Giza pyramid complex is a fraction of the size of his father's and grandfather's pyramids. If Menkaure was so beloved by his people, why is his pyramid so tiny compared to those of Khufu and Khafre? Some Egyptologists suggest that his predecessors "broke the bank" and left Menkaure with little to work with. They suggest that Menkaure directed more resources to creativity and artistry in his mortuary temple and settled for a pyramid of more modest dimensions.

I have an alternate hypothesis. I propose that the three major pyramids, as well as the two subsidiary pyramids and the six "pyramids of the queens" in the Giza pyramid complex, were built long before Djoser tried to imitate them with a step pyramid in Saqqara. I believe that Sneferu also attempted to replicate the great pyramids in Giza by building his step pyramid and bent pyramid in Meidum and his successful pyramid replica in Dahshur.

Then, I imagine that Pharaoh Sneferu's son, Khufu, grandson, Khafre, and great grandson, Menkaure, each chose one of the existing pyramids within the Giza pyramid complex and built their ornate mastabas at the end of each causeway leading away from "their" pyramid and decorated the causeway so that future generations would accredit the construction of the pyramids to them.

This hypothesis better explains why there are no hieroglyphs inside the great pyramids. Additionally, the hieroglyphs on the causeway walls or on the mastabas (crypts) do not describe how the three pharaohs built "their" respective pyramids. Certainly, they would have wanted credit for such amazing feats of architecture. Yet, the only key element in the Giza pyramid complex giving any suggestion that any of the many pharaohs had anything to do with the construction of any of the Giza Pyramids is the Sphinx that now bears the face of a man, whom Egyptologists identify as Pharaoh Khufu. (They insist that his face is on the Sphinx even though not one other depiction of Pharaoh Khufu, nor one description of him, exists for comparison.) My hypothesis is that Khufu, Khafre, and Menkaure did not build the great pyramids in Giza, nor the Sphinx, nor most of the various other components in the complex.

So, if the Giza pyramid complex was built before 3000 BC, when was it built? It could have been built any time before then, but my hypothesis is that the Giza pyramid complex was constructed hundreds of years before the Dynastic Period. I believe that the complex was a fixture in Egypt before Egyptian civilization developed. The Giza complex had been admired by Egyptians for so long (without a human explanation for its existence) that it became the inspiration for the Ancient Egyptian belief system that was used by Menes around 3000 BC to proclaim himself a pharaoh with supernatural powers.

We learn from the Bible that Eve and Adam were convinced by the snake (Satan) in the Garden of Eden that they should covet the knowledge of God and disobey God by eating of the fruit on the Tree of Knowledge. Similarly, if the three largest pyramids in the Giza pyramid complex had been standing for centuries, eventually a king would have wanted to know more about them and perhaps try to replicate their construction. And certainly, a self-proclaimed "god" would have tried to take credit for the pyramids in future, non-witnessing generations. They would have had to be very cunning about how they took such credit, though, because anyone alive during their reign and for many subsequent generations would have, through oral tradition, relayed the fact that Khufu, Khafre, and Menkaure had not built the great pyramids in Giza. In all fairness, Khufu, Khafre, and Menkaure may never have intended to take credit for building of any of the key elements of the Giza pyramid complex. Credit may have been given to them, either knowingly or naively, by their descendants who had become proficient at building smaller pyramids. The fact is that we do not know for certain when the key elements of the Giza pyramid complex were built nor do we know who built them.

There are Coptic and Arabic legends regarding the great pyramids at Giza which suggest that the Khufu Pyramid was built before the Flood to store scientific knowledge and literature so that it would not be lost. According to the Coptic legend, King Surid, who lived three hundred years before the Flood, had had a precognitive dream about the Flood and sealed treasures, art and scientific knowledge within the Khufu Pyramid. According to the Arabic legend, the god Hermes (the Greek version of the Egyptian god Thoth) built the Khufu Pyramid to preserve literature and science from the Flood and to hide the information from "the uninitiated." (The idea that there is literature and science embedded within the Giza pyramid complex turns out to be the core of my hypothesis, as you will learn very soon.)

While writing this book, an important discovery was made. In 2019, Abeer Eladany, a curatorial assistant for the University of Aberdeen Museums (UAM) in Scotland, discovered a cigar tin which had been missing for seventy years. Ms. Eladany had been assigned to review items in the Asian collection when she found the tin and, being of Egyptian descent, recognized the writing on the tin to be Egyptian. When she opened the tin, she found five pieces of cedar. Upon investigation, it was learned that the cedar (originally one 5" long piece that resembled a measuring device with one pointed end), along with a metal double hook and a stone sphere made of dolerite, had been removed from the Khufu Pyramid in 1872 by Waynman Dixon, a British Engineer known for his work on the Great Pyramid. While Waynman Dixon was constructing a bridge in Cairo, Piazzi Smyth asked him to assist with a survey on the Great Pyramid. While Dixon was searching for "air shafts" exiting the "Queen's Chamber", he discovered the three relics. According to museum records, the cedar was in the possession of Dr. James Grant, a Scottish doctor who had been practicing medicine in Egypt and had been present when Dixon located the relics. In 1946, Dr. Grant's daughter presented the tin with the cedar remains to the UAM. Sometime during the next three years, the cedar pieces were misfiled in the Asian collection.

The rediscovered cedar was carbon dated in 2020 and found to have been chopped down at least 500 years before the Great Pyramid is generally believed to have been built. That piece of cedar was chopped down between 3341 BC and 3094 BC (or year 666 on the Hebrew Calendar.) [Interestingly, it is believed that the bases of the crucifixion devices were made of cedar. It is also of note that Sir Isaac Newton believed that the great pyramids at Giza hold the key to the date of the Apocalypse.]

Because the Great Pyramid was built long before Khufu was born, I am thoroughly convinced that neither Khufu, nor Khafre, nor Menkaure built any of the pyramids at Giza. So, if Khufu, Khafre, and Menkaure did not build them, who did?

Chapter 4

Who Did Build The Giza Pyramid Complex?

I am going to keep you waiting a little bit longer before I tell you why the Giza pyramid complex was built. First, I need to tell you who I believe built it. As I stated before, I do believe that human beings participated in the building of the pyramids and other elements in the Giza pyramid complex. However, I do not believe that humans designed the Giza pyramid complex nor did they build it on their own. I believe that ancient human beings had help. So, who helped them?

As I pointed out in the last chapter, pyramids resembling the two largest pyramids in the Giza pyramid complex were never replicated elsewhere. I believe there are three possible explanations for this: a lack of materials, a discontinuity in knowledge of how to build such a large pyramid (technology), or a lack of labor force. The first possible explanation can be eliminated by the fact that a multiple amount of materials were used to build all of the smaller pyramids outside of the Giza pyramid complex. Lack of technology should not have been a factor because, given the dates when most Egyptologists and archaeologists believe the largest pyramids were built (the second completed within about twenty years of the completion of the first and Menkaure's smaller pyramid completed within about thirty years of the second large pyramid), the technology for building large pyramids certainly would have been available to Menkaure.

Hence, I am inclined to attribute the discontinuation of building large pyramids to a lack of labor force. But there is evidence of tremendous numbers of people living very near the Giza pyramid complex for generations. Certainly, there was no lack of people and no lack of food to feed the people, or the civilization would have migrated or evaporated completely. Yet, if the skill set of the pyramid builders changed over time (such as their size or strength), a change in the available labor force would have occurred. Larger, stronger humans could do more, bigger work. In the Book of Genesis, in the Old Testament, in Chapter 6, Verse 4, there is a description of "humans" who were much larger and stronger than humans- Nephilim. Nephilim were the offspring created by the union of the Sons of God (Angels) with the daughters of men. They were much stronger and larger than humans. I suggest that the Nephilim were the primary labor force used to build the larger pyramids at Giza which were attributed to Pharaoh Khufu and Pharaoh Khafre. The humans there, I believe, were the descendants of Cain. (I will explain why I believe they were the descendants of Cain, not Seth, later in this chapter.)

[Before I go any further with the explanation of my hypothesis, I must reiterate that, as I mentioned in the forward to this book, I am not a biblical scholar and only a Bible student. I have also relayed that I am not an archaeologist, anthropologist, or an Egyptologist. I have developed my hypothesis by reviewing documentation from multiple disciplines and by evaluating scholars' generally accepted hypotheses and the detailed evidence they have used to support their hypotheses. My hypothesis is a synthesis of all that I have read and is offered as an alternate hypothesis which may encourage further evaluation and analysis of all information available on the subject of the Giza pyramid complex. I am open to review by anyone.]

I do believe that the Giza pyramid complex, because of the materials from which it was built and its design, definitely could have survived a great flood. I hypothesize that the Giza pyramid complex was built by humans with the help of the Nephilim, with angels as the foremen of the project designed by God. But who were these daughters of man with whom the angels of God procreated to bear Nephilim? Two key male lineages descended from Adam and Eve are named in the Bible: the descendants of Cain and the descendants of Seth. Their second son, Abel, was murdered by Cain before he reproduced. Cain was cast out by God to the east of Eden for this but was protected by a "sign" so that no one would kill him. God does not make a practice of preserving the life of someone who commits evil unless he has a future purpose for them.

We are told, in Genesis 6:4, that the Nephilim were "... the mighty ones of old times, the men of fame." They had offspring until they were wiped out by the Great Flood. However, the creation of Nephilim and their offspring was not attributed to God. In fact, their existence and the misbehavior of the angels responsible for such offspring greatly angered God. However, I believe that God utilized the Nephilim for the construction of the Giza pyramids. Unfortunately, in Genesis 6:5, we are told that man's wickedness caused God to regret having made man and that God decided to wipe man off the face of the earth. And because Noah is descended from Seth with ancestors who dwelled elsewhere, Noah probably had no knowledge of the Nephilim or of the great pyramids. Moses, who descended from Noah's son, Shem, "wrote" the Book of Genesis, (where we are told of the Nephilim) from God's dictation.

According to the Hebrew calendar, the year 5781 is the year (2021 AD), and that sets the birth of man at 3760 BC. So, using the ages of the descendants of Adam when their sons were born, as stated in the Old Testament (Torah), I calculated that the Great Flood occurred 1,656 years after God created Adam. On the Hebrew calendar, that would have been the year 1656, or 2104 BC in the Roman calendar. Depending on whose timeline you accept with regard to the construction of the Great Pyramids, the Khufu and Khafre pyramids were built during the 2500s BC to early 2400s BC. According to the Bible, this would have been before the Great Flood.

Only Noah had God's favor, so when the Great Flood happened, the angels left the earth (per commandment by God) and the Nephilim were wiped off the face of the earth along with nearly all humans with the exception of Noah, his wife, his three sons, and his three daughters-in-law. Eventually, the descendants of Noah's son, Ham (specifically, Noah's grandsons, Put and Mizraim) found their way to Egypt. Put settled in western Egypt, and there is no record of his descendants; however, one of Mizraim's grandsons, Casluhim, was the first generation of the Philistines.

I hypothesize that Mizraim and his people found the Giza pyramid complex when they settled on the fertile ground near the Nile River. In awe, they examined every part of the complex, as human nature would dictate them to do.

In doing so, they discovered documents (perhaps within the red granite "sarcophagus" inside the largest pyramid). They interpreted the documents found and established a religion based on their interpretation of the documents and a culture based on that religion.

[The documents I refer to may have been the knowledge hidden from the uninitiated in the Great Pyramid by King Surid before the Great Flood he had dreamt about, according to Coptic legend. Some suggest that the legend is based on the Torah; however, the Torah, as it is written today, does not mention the Great Pyramid at all.]

Let us consider the similarities between the ancient Egyptian creation story and the Hebrew explanation of creation. Later pyramids (from the late 2100s BC) contain hieroglyphic texts containing three similar, but different cosmologies. One refers to a creator god, Atum, who created eight other gods. (Could this be a reference to Jesus and the seven archangels?) One of the most familiar scenarios depicted in Egyptian art is that of Khnum, the god with the head of a ram, creating a human with clay on his potter's wheel. Then, Khnum breathes life into the nose of his creation. Sound familiar?

However, there is also a polytheistic religion of Egypt which relays the story of two brothers, Osiris and Set. In the story, Set kills Osiris and cuts him into pieces that he scatters. Their sister, Isis, collects the pieces of Osiris' body, reassembles them, and resurrects Osiris with a kiss. Could the descendants of Cain have also left a contradictory story that proclaimed that Cain had been the victim of violence (when he had actually been the perpetrator) and portrayed Cain's brother, Seth, to be the aggressor? Did they depict this story in hieroglyphics, and did Mizraim and his family find this story? Did they also find the Egyptian story of the Sky People who, when they left the earth, anointed certain men to inherit their authority? Nobody can say for certain how long ago these stories became a part of the Egyptian culture. I suggest that, if these stories were left in, or near, the Giza pyramid complex by the descendants of Cain and discovered after the flood by Mizraim, his Hebrew paradigm would have been challenged.

There is also a weaker relationship between Hebrew and Babylonian creation explanations than there is between Hebrew and Egyptian creation explanations. The Book of Genesis describes the first diaspora imposed on humans by God to be from Babel (Babylon). The descendants of Noah were forced to leave Babel because they were building a tower to reach the heavens. God realized that their homogeneity allowed them to stay in one place and challenge His authority together. So, God confused them by creating many languages so that they could not understand each other and humans dispersed to explore the entire Earth.

Thus, if a nomadic group had found the Hebrew creation explanation depicted on stone tablets stored in the red granite sarcophagus in the Khufu Pyramid, what might that have looked like to them? If that group of people had not had access for generations to the Hebrew explanation passed down through oral tradition, those hieroglyphic drawings may have been open to interpretation to whatever degree they now lacked a connection to their ancestors. And if Mizraim and his tribe also discovered the alternate Egyptian creation stories, which would they choose to base their new, isolated civilization on where they lived on fertile ground near the magnificent Giza pyramid complex? Through their alternate reality developed in isolation from their God-serving relatives, they could attribute anything to themselves. They could even attribute the building of the great pyramids and the surrounding complex to the leader of their choosing. After a few generations, only the descendants of the privileged few would know the truth. Everyone else would serve them under their revised truth.

Then, when the descendants of Noah's grandson Canaan arrived, they had a labor force to help the descendants of Mizraim build replicas of the great pyramids in honor of their kings. For generations, the Canaanites were relegated to the servant ("slave") class. So, even though they were to serve the royal class, they would do so in a land with fertile soil. What a perfect setup for a civilization optimal for peaceful domination and submission. Together, they could build pyramids for each king, or pharaoh.

The Egyptian pharaohs are first mentioned in the Old Testament when Abraham, a tenth generation descendant of Noah's son, Shem, took his wife, Sarah, to Egypt because of famine. This time frame would have given the descendants of Mizraim and Canaan about eight generations to have established Egypt and Egyptian civilization with an alternate religion and culture. Abraham and Sarah were not in Egypt long because God struck the pharaoh and his family with plagues and the pharaoh sent Abraham and Sarah away. This unfortunate chain of events was initiated by Abraham's dishonesty, which he felt was necessary to preserve his life. It was a good thing that Abraham and Sarah survived, or Moses would never have been born.

[It should not be difficult to accept the possibility that a new civilization could evolve within seven or eight generations. During the time I have been alive, I have shared life experiences with five generations of fellow human beings. So many things that my grandparents experienced using in daily life are unavailable, and even unfathomable to the generation being born today. Even though I have photographs and film and books to show the youngest generation when I refer to things "from the old days," they cannot imagine the experience of using those things. Those things, their usefulness, and how they were made will be forgotten soon. Just imagine how much easier it would have been to "erase" memories that had not been documented in hieroglyphs commissioned by the ruling class in ancient Egypt.]

I also give as an example the modern cellular phone. A modern smart phone has more functionality and more memory than the computer I am using to write this book. In fact, a cell phone has ten times the capacity of this computer! How many young people care to understand the iterations it took to create the cell phone they use? Not many. However, they certainly know how to use the cell phone and would not want to live without it. So, when Mizraim and his people came upon the Giza pyramid complex and the fertile soil surrounding it, I doubt they stopped to analyze how they were built. They probably inspected the elements of the complex to see how they could serve them. They may have learned that the large shape of the pyramids, resembling mountains, attracted much needed rain which could be directed, in a more controlled fashion, through the causeways to be used for survival. Then, after the Canaanites showed up, they had a labor force to build more pyramids.

The next time Egyptian pharaohs are mentioned in the Old Testament is when Joseph, son of Jacob (Israel), great grandson of Abraham, and the 13th generation descendant of Noah, is taken from his family to Egypt and raised there. Joseph is treated well by the pharaoh and given a high status because of his foresight to store food ahead of a seven year famine. During that famine, Joseph's brothers went to Egypt for food. After the surreptitious interactions Joseph staged so that he could be reunited with his long lost twin, Joseph invited his entire family to take residence in Egypt. Jacob and his descendants lived in peace there for three more generations.

Then, because the Hebrew population had multiplied greatly in Egypt, a new pharaoh decided to slow them down by ordering the slaughter of all Hebrew first born sons. Luckily, the infant Moses' mother put him in a basket and sent him down the Nile River into the path of the pharaoh's daughter. And luckily, the pharaoh's daughter had compassion for the baby and raised Moses as her own. If she hadn't, the truth might have been lost since Moses was the author of the Book of Genesis (as well as other books in the Torah/Old Testament/Hebrew Bible).

I apologize to those of you who are better Bible students than I am for the watered down history lesson. I wanted to get to a very important point: God had a very specific plan in mind that included some intricate twists and turns which could have ended in knots... but the plan was realized. Noah's descendants were dispersed. They found their way to Egypt and subsequent generations made their way to Egypt with the Hebrew tradition. When the descendants of Abraham were no longer welcome in Egypt, God helped Moses lead them out of Egypt. After numerous challenges, God spoke to Moses and Moses gave those words to future generations. Moses did not give us the Egyptian creation story (which he certainly would have heard) documented in Egyptian hieroglyphics (which he certainly would have used); and he did not mention pyramids (which he certainly would have seen). By the time Moses wrote the Books in the Torah, he had been visited by God (in the form of a burning bush) and had been given the Ten Commandments by God. Wouldn't God have corrected any errors in Moses' mind as to the true story of man's creation? Certainly, He would have. And Moses, being a true servant of God, would never have perpetuated a false story of creation by God. Moses gave us God's Truth.

As a student of God's Truth, I see the connection between the historical events relayed in this chapter and the patterns in the construction of pyramids in Egypt and I must conclude that the Giza pyramid complex was not built by the descendants of Ham. The Giza pyramid complex was built by the descendants of Cain with the physical help of the Nephilim and the technical guidance of God's angels to complete God's design. The Giza pyramid complex was part of God's plan; otherwise, it would have been wiped off the face of the Earth during the Great Flood. I choose to believe that the complex was built under the direction of God for His purpose. And now, I can present my hypothesis for why the Giza pyramid complex was built.

Quite surprisingly, the minute I finished writing this chapter, my co-author found a book titled, *Our Inheritance In The Great Pyramid*, written in 1874 by Piazzi Smyth. Piazzi Smyth dedicated his book to his friend, John Taylor, who authored the book titled, *The Great Pyramid; Why Was It Built, and Who Built It?* In the Preface to Smyth's book, he explains that his research pathway coincided with that of Taylor, but that he felt he needed to go to Egypt to take better measurements of the Great Pyramid. Smyth's four month residence near the Great Pyramid produced his three volume book, *Life and Work at the Great Pyramid in 1865*. By trade, Smyth was an astronomer and took very detailed measurements of every aspect of the Great Pyramid. What may strike you as hard as it did me, are the allusions Smyth made about why, or the purpose of, the Great Pyramid (which he painstakingly measured more than 150 years ago) and who had a hand in building it.

Before his Preface to *Our Inheritance In The Great Pyramid*, Piazzi Smyth quoted Jeremiah 32:18-20:

> The great, the mighty God, the Lord of Hosts, is His name, great in counsel, and mighty in work; ... which hast set signs and wonders in the land of Egypt, even unto this day.

And, in his Preface to the same, Smyth writes:

> ...the Great Pyramid, though *in* Egypt is not *of* Egypt; and though built in the earliest ages of man upon earth, far before all history, was yet prophetically intended to subserve a high purpose for these days in which we live and the coming days. That it, the Great Pyramid, has never been even remotely understood yet by any race of men, though it has been a standing riddle guessed at by all of them in their successive ages; but that it is able nevertheless to tell its own story and explain its mission most unmistakably: not indeed by reference to, or use of, any written language, whether hieroglyphic or vulgar, -but by aid of the mathematical and physical science of *modern times*: a means fore-ordained both for preventing the parable being read too soon in the history of the world, and for insuring its being correctly read by all nations when the fullness of time shall have arrived.
>
> ...the Great Pyramid. Which building is moreover an earlier document in the history of the human race; while the putting together of its stones into the vocal and deeply-meaning shapes we see them in now, was absolutely contemporary with the first of the primeval events to which it was destined to bear indubitable witness in these latter days, and not sooner.

So, I am not the first person interested in the Giza pyramid complex who believes that God had had a hand in the construction of the Great Pyramids.

Thirty-seven years before Piazzi Smyth wrote the book I quoted, Colonel Howard Vyse wrote *Operations Carried On At The Pyramids of Gizeh In 1837: With An Account Of A Voyage Into Upper Egypt And An Appendix.* On page 48 of Volume II, he writes as a footnote:

> The mode of burial in a plain sarcophagus deposited in a pyramid without inscription, or sculpture, is so directly contrary to that usually practised by the Egyptians, in which not only the sarcophagus, but also the whole of the building were covered with hieroglyphics, that both of them can hardly be supposed to have been used by the same people. It seems probable, therefore, that the former was adopted by those mighty strangers, who, according to the most authentic accounts, had possession of Egypt at a very remote period, but not before hieroglyphics had been invented, and the arts had arrived at great excellence, which might well be the case, as we know, from sacred history, that science flourished before the deluge.

Hieroglyphic records of the construction of the Giza pyramid complex have never been discovered. Why not? A tremendous amount of coordination would have been necessary to complete such a large project. There would have been labor to manage; production and distribution of food for the labor to coordinate; and the extraction and transportation of materials from their source locations to Giza would have been documented as it had been for other pyramid projects. Elaborate systems of these sorts are imperative when each person involved in a project has a specialized role. Perhaps there was no specialization involved in the construction of the Giza pyramid complex. If each participant was capable of completing any task necessary to complete the project, a simple method of rotating people from one task to the next on a schedule would suffice to manage the project. No record keeping would be needed, no managers would be needed, and everyone could be equally devoted to the completion of the project. No hierarchy would be required. Only sons of God, or humans with perfect bodies, could have completed such a project with such efficiency and without disharmony.

In this possible scenario, it may have been during this project that the sons of God became enamored with the daughters of men and created the Nephilim. The big and strong Nephilim may have been used to do physical labor faster than humans and, eventually, replaced humans. Hence, specialization of roles and the creation of hierarchies began. Competition for the prized roles in the new social system and oppression of the masses by the strongest few would have become the norm quickly. I believe that, because hierarchy created disharmony and corruption, God was so displeased with humans that He sent the Great Flood.

Although the published works I have quoted are out of print and difficult to acquire, they exist and should not be ignored. These authors' drawings are often used in more re-cent authors' books (including this book); however, Smyth's and Vyse's hypotheses are not expounded, and are sometimes even discredited. I believe this is due to the generally accept-ed 20th century viewpoint that science and religion can not both be true. I have made it clear that I believe that both can be true, and there is a contemporary trend towards such. If you are on board with me and consider that God directed the building of elements of the Giza pyramid complex, you will appreciate my hypothesis as to why I believe God did so.

Hannah Anderson

Chapter 5

Why the Giza Pyramid Complex Was Built

As a curious human, I feel that the most important question to be answered about any subject is, "why?" Yet you cannot answer that question without identifying what, when, and who. I have presented the case for my hypothesis that the Giza pyramid complex was not built to be a burial chamber. I have stated that the complex could have survived the Great Flood; and thus, it could have been built any time before 2105 BC. And I revealed that, as a Bible student, I would give credit for the construction of the complex to God and His angels. So, I am finally ready to tell you my hypothesis for why the Giza pyramid complex was built.

As I mentioned in the last chapter, I serendipitously uncovered a book titled, *Our Inheritance In The Great Pyramid*, written by Piazzi Smyth, a Scottish astronomer, in 1874. Piazzi Smyth was influenced by the work of Colonel Howard Vyse, who wrote a two volume work titled, *The Pyramids of*

Gizeh. The complete title is: *Operations Carried On At The Pyramids of Gizeh In 1837: With An Account Of A Voyage Into Upper Egypt, And An Appendix*. Their conclusions were disputed by other researchers and Egyptologists, as I fully expect my work to be, because we three credit God for the design of the Great Pyramid. Smyth also gave similar importance to certain design elements of the Great Pyramid that I will describe for you soon. I plan to quote some of Smyth's and Vyse's writings in this chapter, not as evidence that my hypothesis is correct regarding the Giza pyramid complex, but because I am human and their expansive research (done about 150 and 185 years ago) gives me a sense of confirmation and validity.

Perhaps Smyth presented his hypothesis too soon, and now is a more appropriate time to consider such possibilities. For example, interest in the study of human behavior is a 20th century phenomenon and the disciplines of Social Psychology and Socio-cultural Anthropology were unavailable to Smyth to use as a lens for analysis. Fortunately for me, I was raised by a mechanical engineer and my co-author was raised by a social psychologist, a researcher who was raised by a Baptist Minister with a degree in Theology. Additionally, because neither of us pursued a specialized higher education much beyond a Bachelor's Degree, we are free to explore the contributions that multiple disciplines provide to my hypothesis without being disloyal to any one of them. Hence, my hypothesis is ultimately a synthesis of my enhanced, but limited, understanding of every discipline I saw fit to include in this analysis.

I have tremendous respect for Piazzi Smyth, who seemed to have no issue with combining scientific research with biblical purpose at a time when the schism between science and religion was pronounced. Even within my lifetime, it is only recently that I have been able to mention both within a conversation without offending everyone present. The divide still exists, but I hope that my hypothesis will help narrow it.

Remember that, in his Preface to *Our Inheritance In The Great Pyramid*, Piazzi Smyth wrote,

> ...the Great Pyramid, though *in* Egypt is not *of* Egypt; and though built in the earliest ages of man upon earth, far before all history, was yet prophetically intended to subserve a high purpose for these days in which we live and the coming days. That it, the Great Pyramid, has never been even remotely understood yet by any race of men, though it has been a standing riddle guessed at by all of them in their successive ages; but that it is able nevertheless to tell its own story and explain its mission most unmistakably: not indeed by reference to, or use of, any written language, whether hieroglyphic or vulgar- but by aid of mathematical and physical science of *modern times*: a means fore-ordained both for preventing the parable being read too soon in the history of the world, and for insuring its being correctly read by all nations when the fulness of time shall have arrived.

Unfortunately for Smyth, I believe that his hypothesis was presented 150 years too soon. I may learn that my similar hypothesis is still too difficult for many to receive, yet I will present it now.

I hypothesize that the Giza pyramid complex was designed by God and constructed by humans and their stepbrothers, the Nephilim, with God's angels as foremen. After twenty years of analyzing others' measurements and diagrams of the complex from the inside, from the outside, and from above, I began to see patterns in its design. During the last eight years of my research, I have sought mathematical, geometric, and trigonometric evidence to support my hypothesis. When the numbers did not fit the hypothesis, I reorganized my hypothesis to match my findings. I realize that my method does not fit the accepted scientific method as used by scientists; however, as I admitted, I am not a scientist. Additionally, my research and hypothesis reaches out into multiple disciplines, some of which do not embrace the scientific method.

Is it possible that God has provided us with a path to salvation, both physical and spiritual, for our species? If so, are the tools we will need to achieve salvation described, inscribed, and prescribed throughout the world in oral tradition and writing, as well as in physical structures designed by nature and by man? I believe that the Giza pyramid complex is one such set of physical structures which can be used as a tool to achieve physical and spiritual salvation in the not so distant future. What kind of tool?

I hypothesize that the Giza pyramid complex is a map (or a cairn, if you will). It is a map that recounts key moments of our history and aids us with direction to where we want to go (as most maps do). This special map also provides guidance through key moments and destinations in our prophesied future. Welcome aboard my multi-disciplinary tour of the Giza pyramid complex. I will present you with mathematical, geometric, and trigonometric evidence that the complex depicts certain aspects of our origins and of our future, as told in the Bible, in a form which is not bound by language, time, culture, or religion.

Chapter 6

Design of the Giza Pyramid Complex

As is true of any map, the design of this map follows an accepted recipe. There is a compass, a legend, and other elements which are consistent in their presentation. Traditional detailed maps become obsolete once too many additions are made to the areas they are attempting to guide you through. The Giza pyramid complex is a unique map in that it was designed so that it could not be properly "read" until the time was ripe for it to be read. In order to be able to read the Giza pyramid complex, humans had to develop the necessary interest, technology, and spiritual awareness.

The interest in the complex as a source of knowledge, rather than a source of materials to be robbed and sold to the highest bidder, began in the eighteen hundreds AD. As Piazzi Smyth wrote:

> This spread of purely-obtained Great Pyramid information, unalloyed by the Cainite profanities of

Pharaonic Egypt...brought by degrees several able intellectualists into the field... And there are even some most interesting and hopeful circumstances in the evolution of the scientific contents of the Great Pyramid just now, causing the present time to be almost the beginning of a new era of increased certainty and more precise knowledge regarding all that that ancient building was originally intended for; and which certainly includes much of the sacred, as well as the secular.

To be certain, the Giza pyramid complex had attracted the curiosity and intrigue of all who saw it after the fall of the Ancient Egyptian Empire to the Nubians around 728 BC. Because other, much smaller, pyramids had been built and their construction had been documented by the pharaohs' historians, the construction of the Giza pyramid complex was attributed to earlier pharaohs.

However, it was not until Smyth's friend, Taylor, first measured the largest pyramid in the complex that a purpose for its construction was surmised to be other than what was previously accepted. Piazzi Smyth (intrigued by Taylor's hypothesis, yet dissatisfied with how Taylor had measured the Great Pyramid) went to Egypt to survey the pyramid with more modern tools. This approach was preferable to others' attempts to examine the pyramids in the complex by blasting holes through internal walls, or worse. [At the end of the 12th century AD, a Kurdish, Suni Muslim, who was the son of the Egyptian Sultan Saladin, initiated an unsuccessful attempt to disassemble the smaller Menkaure Pyramid.]

As ever more modern tools became available, such as aerial imagery and ground penetrating radar, more detailed measurements and drawings of the Giza pyramid complex have been made available. Some of the most useful diagrams for my research were provided by William Matthew Flinders Petrie in his *The Pyramids and Temples of Gizah*, published in 1883. By profession, Petrie was a surveyor, so his renderings were the most accurate until the Giza Plateau Computer Model was compiled by the University of Chicago under the direction of Dr. Mark Lehner, beginning in 1997. Some of the renderings appear in Dr. Mark Lehner's book, *The Complete Pyramids*, published in 1999. Most of my numerical research was completed using renderings from these two sources.

Everything In Its Place

As you can see in my diagram (Plate 6-1), drawn from an aerial perspective, there is a geometric order to the Giza pyramid complex with a prominent cardinal north/south alignment. [I will use

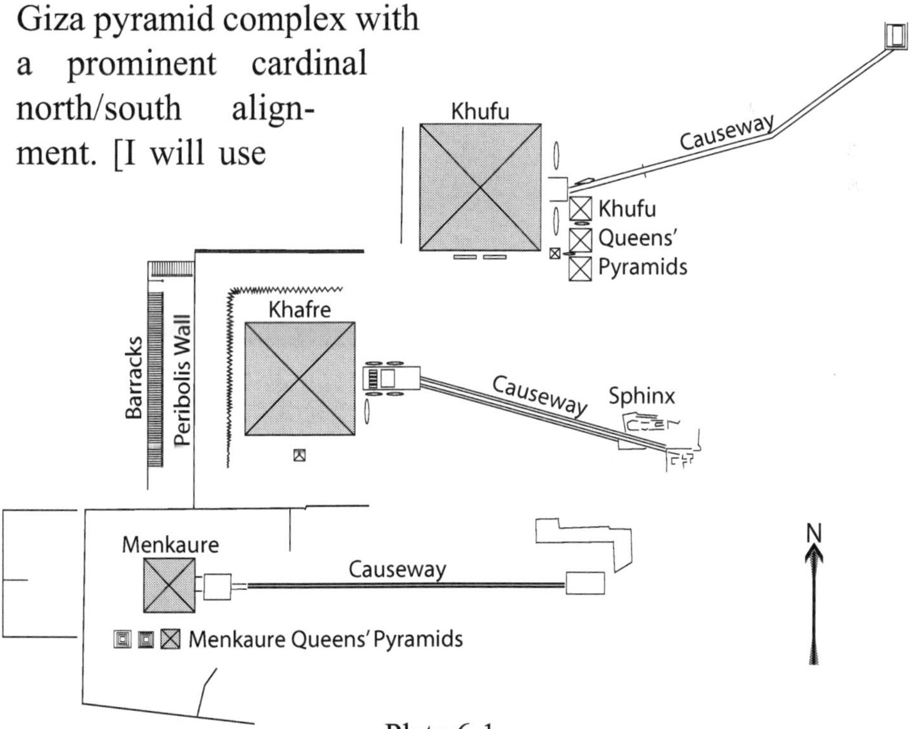

Plate 6-1

the names for each element of the complex, as referred to by Petrie or Lehner, for the sake of simplicity.] The three Great Pyramids are the most prominent features of the complex. There is one colossal pyramid (Khufu Pyramid), a very large pyramid (Khafre Pyramid), and a small pyramid (Menkaure Pyramid) in a diagonal formation from northeast to southwest. (In fact, the Khufu Pyramid and Khafre Pyramid are almost perfectly aligned along their diagonals.) There is a mortuary temple to the east of each of the three pyramids and a causeway leading away from each mortuary temple at different angles; and each causeway terminates at a valley temple.

To the east of the Khufu Pyramid, south of the beginning of the causeway, there are three small subsidiary pyramids, of about the same dimensions, in a line from north to south. To the south of the center of the southern face of the Khafre Pyramid, is a very small pyramid. And, south of the southern face of the Menkaure Pyramid, beginning slightly east of center and continuing west, there are three small pyramids of differing dimensions.

Also to the east of the Khufu Pyramid, there are five boat pits in different orientations to the pyramid (refer to Plate 6-2). There is one boat pit on each side of the mortuary temple, parallel to the east face of the pyramid. A third boat pit is parallel to the beginning of the causeway. A smaller, fourth boat pit is between the northernmost and center subsidiary pyramids. And the smallest, fifth boat pit is located between the center and southmost subsidiary pyramids. Half of this last boat pit extends toward a tiny subsidiary pyramid located at the southeast corner of the Khufu pyramid. To the east of the Khafre Pyramid, there are also five boat pits. Four of the boat pits are the same size: two are aligned parallel and north of the mortuary temple, while the other two are

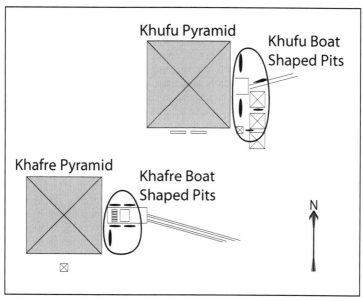

Plate 6-2

south of the mortuary temple. The fifth boat pit is larger than the others and is south of the mortuary temple and aligned parallel to the Khafre Pyramid. There are no boat pits near the Menkaure Pyramid.

There is a system of what have been called "work-men's barracks" by many Egyptologists, even though there is no evidence that anyone has ever lived there. Lehner de-scribes them as being so precise in their dimensions that they resemble a comb. Petrie, before him, also noted their precise dimensions and referred to them as galleries. They are lo-cated to the west of the Khafre Pyramid beyond the Peribolus Wall (see Plate 6-3). The galleries were built of rough pieces of limestone with hard mud floors. At the northernmost end, running east to west, there are 17 galleries, and running north to south (perpendicular to the last five galleries) there are 73 galleries.

The system of walls in the Giza pyramid complex will be a part of my later discussion. What I wish to point out

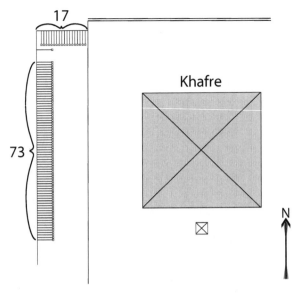

Plate 6-3

now is that, typically, the purpose of walls is to provide protection. The Peribolus Wall protects the Khafre Pyramid to the west, and another wall protects it to the north. There are walls to the north, west, and south of the Menkaure Pyramid. The prevailing winds blow from the north. To the west lies the desert. The sun rises in the east and the Nile River is there.

The infamous Sphinx is located to the northwest of the valley temple at the end of the Khafre Pyramid causeway. The Sphinx faces due east as if guarding the Giza pyramid complex or greeting the sunrise.

All of these elements within the Giza pyramid complex were used in my research. I evaluated the measurements of each element, their orientation in relationship to other elements, their angularities without and within, and the qualities and quantities of their sub-elements. The elements I have not yet evaluated are not necessarily unimportant. In fact, I suspect that every detail of each element is important. However, I was able to support my hypothesis to my satisfaction with the elements I did analyze.

In the six chapters that follow, I will explain how I have concluded that the Giza pyramid complex was built to serve future humans (perhaps us) as a computer, a galactic map, a non-literary transmission of the Word of God, and a revelatory devise for determining the fate of humankind.

The Great Pyramid (Khufu), Descending Passage Entrance

Operations Carried On At the Pyramids Of Gizeh in 1837 Vol. 1, 1840
Howard-R Vyse

Chapter 7

The Giza Pyramid Complex Computer

By meticulously examining every element within the complex, I came to the conclusion that elements of the Giza pyramid complex can be used as a computer. I have considered each dimension, every angle, the distances between each element, and the orientations of each element with regard to other elements. In the next chapter, I will explain how the Giza pyramid complex computer can be used to interpret the Giza pyramid complex galactic map. Every map requires a legend, and the most useful tool in the legend is the measurement unit. In this chapter, I will explain how I discovered the measurement units for distance and time which are embedded in the Giza pyramid complex.

What originally caught my attention is the fact that one of the boat pits east of the Khufu pyramid was in a different orientation to the pyramid than the other four there. This boat pit is north of, and aligns parallel to, the causeway, indicating the potential to travel down the causeway. This led me to consider that the causeways may be symbols of directions of travel.

I examined the other causeways in the complex and I noticed that the causeway exiting the Khafre Pyramid reflects the causeway exiting the Khufu pyramid. In other words, if one were to draw a straight line perpendicular to the east side of each pyramid, the causeway exiting the Khufu Pyramid diverts north at the same angle as the causeway exiting the Khafre Pyramid diverts south. This caught my attention. So, I extended both of the causeways to the west (Plate 7-1) and the extended lines intersect at the barracks near the west wall. (The exact location of the intersection point is significant as well, and I will reveal the significance of this soon.)

If the causeways are symbolic of travel, I thought,

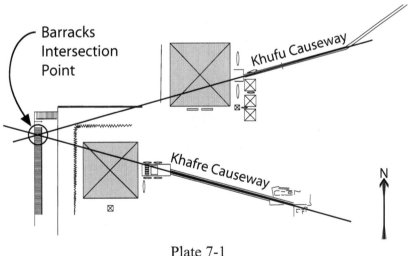

Plate 7-1

where are they indicating travel to? To calculate where in space the complex was indicating, I needed a unit of measurement that would be constant over time and significant to humans. The most reliable measurement I could come up with is the average distance from the Earth to the Sun (one astronomical unit, or AU). So, I made many comparisons between the elements of the complex until I found one which referenced this measurement called an astronomical unit.

I finally found the astronomical unit encoded in the complex by using Lehner's measurements of the angles of ascension of the sides of the Khufu, Khafre, and Menkaure Pyramids. The angle of ascension to the top of the Khufu Pyramid is 51 degrees, 50 minutes, and 40 seconds; the angle of ascension to the top of the Khafre Pyramid is 53 degrees and 10 minutes; and the angle of ascension to the top of the Menkaure Pyramid is 51 degrees, 20 minutes, and 25 seconds. When I compared the angle of ascension of one pyramid to each of the other two, I got three significant results. The angle of ascension to the top of the Khafre Pyramid minus the angle of ascension to the top of the Khufu Pyramid equals 1 degree, 19 minutes, and 20 seconds. If you build a right triangle (see Plate 7-2) with this difference being one of the angles and the second being a right angle, the third angle would be 88 degrees, 40 minutes, and 40 seconds. If you designate the point where the right angle is as the Sun, and the point where the third angle is as the Earth, and the distance between them to be one astronomical unit, the distance from the Sun to the first point (Khafre-Khufu) can be determined (using trigonometry) to be 43.325 astronomical units. This happens to be approximately the distance light travels in one quarter of an Earth rotation (6 hours). One complete Earth

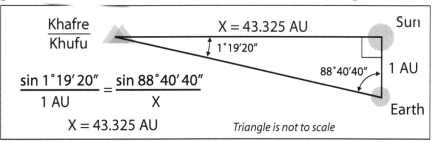

Plate 7-2

rotation is 360 degrees, and one quarter of an Earth rotation equals 90 degrees. To complete this calculation, one must use the speed of light, which was evaluated by Michelson in 1920, about one hundred years ago.

This discovery could not have been the result of a co-incidence. Because one quarter of an Earth rotation equals 90 degrees (a right angle), we have a coordinate system with four quadrants represented to us. Additionally, this representation is presented using the two largest pyramids in the complex in order to indicate the significance of this discovery.

So, I performed the same set of calculations comparing the angle of ascension to the top of the Khafre Pyramid to the angle of ascension to the top of the Menkaure Pyramid with a result of 31.36 astronomical units (see Plate 7-3). This measurement is approximately equivalent to the distance from

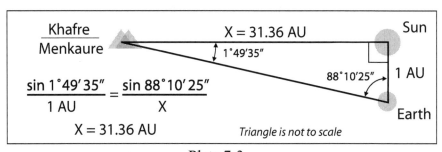

Plate 7-3

the Sun to the outermost planet in the solar system: Neptune. [Pluto lost its planet status in August of 2006.] And, when I made the same comparison between Khufu and Menkaure and performed the corresponding calculations, the result was 113.64 astronomical units (see Plate 7-4). This measurement approximately represents the distance from the Sun at which the effect of the solar wind dissipates (called the heliopause). [Astronomers observed this phenomenon in August of 2013 when Voyager I entered interstellar space, and again in November 2018 when Voyager II did the same.]

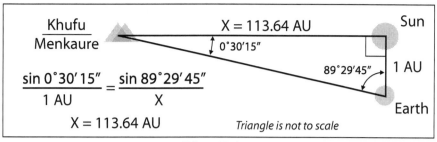

Plate 7-4

After completing these calculations, I became aware of Petrie's *The Pyramids and Temples of Gizeh*. I was able to borrow the first edition of the book from the Stanford University library; however, I was able to purchase a copy of the edition of the book that had been revised by Dr. Zahi Hawass, an Egyptian Egyptologist. Unfortunately, the revised edition did not include half of the original plates, some of which I felt were important. Fortunately, I later acquired a digital copy of the original book. I mention this because one of the missing plates, the original Plate 4, held the information I needed for my next calculations.

In Plate 7-5, you can see that to the west of the Khafre

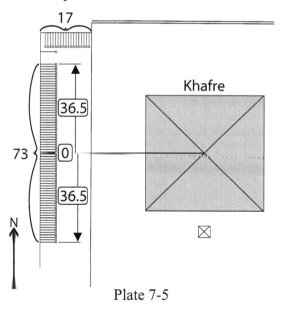

Plate 7-5

Pyramid, beyond the west Peribolus Wall, is a row of what Petrie called, "galleries" and Lehner called "workmen's barracks." There are 73 evenly spaced barracks, the center of which is halfway between the 36th and 37th barracks, and is in line with the apex of the Khafre Pyramid. This orientation of these two structures and the ruler-like appearance of the barracks attracted my attention, so I further examined the row of barracks and its potential numerical significance. I also noticed that the total length of the 73 barracks appeared to be similar to the length of the diagonal of the base of the Khufu Pyramid (The Great Pyramid). (This comparison was easier to make with an aerial view.) Using the Pythagorean Theorem and the length of a side of the square base of the pyramid, I was able to calculate the length of the hypotenuse/diagonal of the base of the Khufu Pyramid (Plate 7-6).

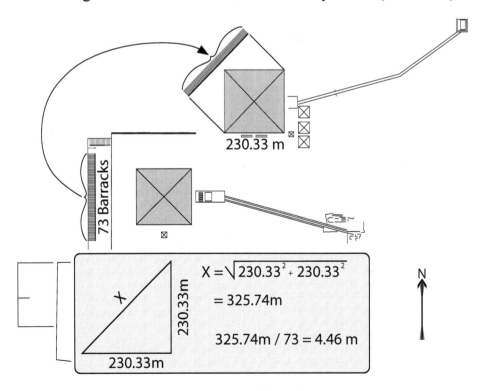

$$X = \sqrt{230.33^2 + 230.33^2}$$

$$= 325.74\,m$$

$$325.74\,m / 73 = 4.46\,m$$

Plate 7-6

Amazingly, the result was equivalent to the distance from one end to the other of the 73 workmen's barracks. By dividing this total distance by 73 (the number of barracks in this "ruler"), I came up with a "Giza Unit" which measures 4.46 meters. The Giza Y Unit (gy) is the scale I used henceforth to measure anything in a north to south (or y-axis) orientation.

To create a Giza X Unit for a gx scale, I logically used the barracks, at the north end of the "ruler," which lie in a west to east orientation. I noticed that the distance from the west Peribolus Wall to the west wall of the 73 north to south barracks seemed equivalent to the length of the parallel base walls of the Menkaure Pyramid. [Unfortunately, Petrie ran into difficulties when he tried to measure the base of the Menkaure Pyramid. In the end, he did relay that the base is rectangular, yet it is unclear as to which are the "long" and "short" sides of the pyramid. Hence, I used Lehner's measurements of the Menkaure Pyramid to create the gx scale.] I confirmed the validity of my process later, when I discovered what the Menkaure Pyramid represents in the galactic map, which the Giza pyramid complex is. What is important for now is the numerical relationship (a ratio) between the gy scale and the gx scale, which calculates to 0.733:1 (y:x) or 1:1.36 (x:y). If you are interested in my complete mathematical process, you may refer to Appendix A (however, I would wait until later to read it).

I returned to a deeper analysis of the causeways leading to and from the mortuary temples to the east of each of the three primary pyramids. The causeway connected to Menkaure's mortuary temple runs perpendicular to the east. However, the causeways leading to and from the Khufu and Khafre mortuary temples each run at an approximate 15 degree angle. The Khufu causeway runs to the northeast at an approximate 15 degree angle off perpendicular, and the

Khafre causeway runs to the southeast at the same angle off perpendicular. Unless the mastabas to the south of the Khufu causeway were installed before the causeway, there is no reason why the causeway could not have run perpendicular to the Khufu mortuary temple. And, there is absolutely no reason why the Khafre causeway could not have run perpendicular to the Khafre mortuary temple. So, why do these two causeways run at opposite, and equal angles from their respective mortuary temples?

As I mentioned earlier, when I extended both causeways until the extension lines intersected, they did intersect at the north to south barracks wall within the 68th barrack (if counted from south to north), or the 6th barrack (if counted from north to south). Instead, I used the center barrack (la-

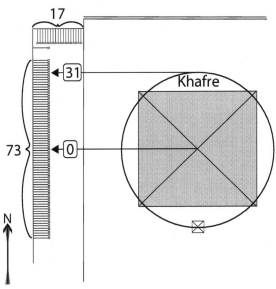

Plate 7-7

beled "0" in Plate 7-5) and counted north to the 31st barrack (see Plate 7-7). (Because the center, or midway between the 36th and 37th barracks, is in perfect alignment with the centerline and apex of the Khafre Pyramid, I decided that the most significant way to interpret the intersection point of the lines extended off the Khufu and Khafre causeways is to indicate that it lies at the 31st barrack north.) Amazed, I noticed that the number 31 is approximately equal to 30.37; and 30.37 astronomical units is the approximate distance from the Sun to Neptune (which we found embedded in the calculation in Plate 7-3 comparing the angles of ascent of the Khafre and Menkaure pyramids). Additionally, a circle with a radius of 31 gy units and its center at the apex of the Khafre Pyramid passes through the apex of its subsidiary pyramid (also on Plate 7-7). I believe that this indicates that the Khafre Pyramid represents our solar system.

Next, I wondered about the significance of the wall that was built between the east to west barracks and the north to south barracks. The wall is parallel to, in alignment with, and the same length as the walls separating all of the north to south barracks, yet it is an unequal distance from the north wall of the northernmost barrack in the "ruler." This indicated to me that this wall is somehow a part of the north to south "ruler." So, I measured how many more barracks (Giza units) would fit into the gap between this wall and the northernmost wall of the north to south "ruler" and I found that five more barracks would fit there. If I were to add five barracks to the number of barracks north of the center of the "ruler" (36.5), I would get 41.5. Interestingly, 41.5 is a close approximation equal to the number of astronomical units for a photon leaving the Sun to travel during the time it takes for the Earth to perform a quarter Earth rotation. (Remember that I received the result of 43.325 astronomical units when I performed the series of calculations in Plate 7-2 comparing the angles of ascent of the Khufu and Khafre pyramids.)

The significance of this is that comparisons of the elements of the Giza pyramid complex can be used to represent distances and can be used to represent lengths of time: two factors needed for directions. Thus, we have a legend containing a scale to compare the distances between elements in the map and the actual distances between the celestial bodies represented by the elements. And, the builders of the complex were kind enough to provide secondary checks on the mathematical calculations needed to solve for distances and times. Because the unit of measurement for distance appears to be the astronomical unit, and the time unit measurement relates to one astronomical unit, the Giza pyramid complex is not an Earth map- it is a galactic map!

Piazzi Smyth also believed that the Pyramids contained a mathematically coded message to be decoded in the latter days. I wonder if Smyth, being an astronomer, suspected that the Great Pyramid was a part of a galactic map.

Chapter 8

The Giza Pyramid Complex Galactic Map

In this chapter, I will show you how I used the "legend" I explained in the last chapter to "read" the galactic map embedded in the Giza pyramid complex. Until very recently, I could not have presented the hypothesis that the Giza pyramid complex is a galactic map. The understanding of geometry and astronomy needed to do so has been evolving for some time. In order to "see" the map embedded in the Giza pyramid complex, I depended heavily on **Starry Night Pro** (professional astronomy telescope control software with a deep sky database). This expansive level of information about our galaxy, and beyond, was first made accessible as software I could use on my laptop computer about twenty years ago (soon after I began my research).

I was able to create a legend for the galactic map, using the calculations described in the previous chapter, containing a scale relating the distances between celestial bodies with respect to time. However, I needed to add a third dimension to my galactic map. To create a three dimensional map, I used the fact that Petrie recognized that, if the Khufu Pyramid is converted into a cone with a circle base having a circumference equal to the total lengths of the sides of the pyramid, the radius of the base of the cone is equal to the height of the pyramid. This fact suggested to me that the x-axis or y-axis coordinates would be equal to their corresponding z-axis coordinates in a three dimensional galactic map. I chose the y-axis coordinates to represent latitude, because y figures are consistent across multiple longitudes; and I chose the x-axis coordinates to represent distances associated with longitude which vary over latitudes. (See Appendix B for a complete explanation.)

I should point out here that, because the pinnacle of the Menkaure Pyramid had eroded by the time Lehner surveyed the pyramid, he gave the measurements for the angles of assent from each side of the base to the apex as equal, even though they could not have been because the base of the pyramid is rectangular. Lehner also estimated the height of the Menkaure Pyramid to be 65 meters. Because he could not have used his numbers to calculate accurately the height of the pyramid, I used the cone base radius to height formula to see if I could accurately calculate the original height of the Menkaure Pyramid, and the result was equivalent to his estimate. I had to use a very convoluted and complex series of calculations using the average of the radii formed by a cone using the "long" and "short" sides of the base of the Menkaure Pyramid. This led me to wonder if the builders of the Giza pyramids had designed the pyramids with the cone base radius formula in mind. Although a conical geometric figure may provide more precise dimensions for calculating the center of the figure, a pyramidal building would withstand the elements much better than a conical building.

Now that I had more accurate dimensions for each of the pyramids, I could figure out what each of the elements in the Giza pyramid complex represents. Because the north-to-south barracks, which represent the Giza Unit scale, are next to and in central alignment with the Khafre Pyramid, I believe that it represents something very significant. The base of the Khafre Pyramid is made of dark granite, which indicates to me that it represents something solid, or long-lasting. Also, if you apply the cone base radius formula to the Khafre Pyramid, the result is far different from its height; thus, the z-axis is not equal to the y-axis. More so, I believe that this indicates that this pyramid represents "here" rather than "out there"; such that, it represents a point on the x-y plane. It can easily be observed that the Khafre Pyramid is in the center of the complex; and so, I logically interpreted it to represent our solar system with the Sun at its center. The plane of the Earth's orbit around the Sun, the ecliptic, is the plane I used as the reference plane with the Sun as a reference point from which to locate and identify other bodies represented by the other elements in the Giza pyramid complex and their relative locations.

Next, I explored the Menkaure Pyramid and its surrounding elements. Using the 73 workmen's barracks as a ruler, I noticed that, by extending the ruler once more to the south, I ended in the center of the Menkuare subsidiary pyramids (their centers being in alignment). Because the easternmost Menkaure subsidiary pyramid is the only perfectly pyramidal of the three subsidiary pyramids (the other two are step pyramids), I deduced that the point represented by this pyramid is the most significant. Additionally, a line drawn north through its center bisects the east-to-west workmen's barracks (which represent the x-axis). This being the case, I designated the center of the easternmost Menkaure subsidiary pyramid to be the point with the three dimensional coordinates (0, 0, 0). I used this point to measure the distance to other elements in the Giza pyramid complex.

Using the Khafre Pyramid as the central point on the plane of reference and the workmen's barracks as the ruler, I determined that the distance due north between the center of the Khafre Pyramid and the easternmost Menkaure subsidiary pyramid is 73 Giza-y Units (gy) plus 36.5 gy, or 109.5

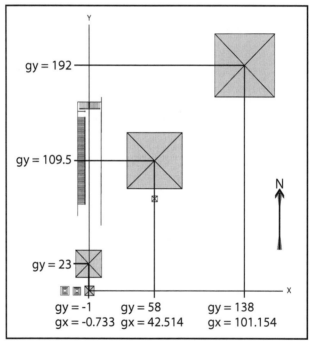

Plate 8-1

gy. (Refer to Plate 8-1.) By using the ratio of the gy scale to the gx scale, which is 0.733:1, and the value of gz as zero (because this point is on the plane of origin), I was able to determine the coordinates for the galactic body represented by the Khafre Pyramid to be (42.514, 109.5, 0). I then measured the distance due north from the center of the easternmost Menkaure subsidiary pyramid to the center of the

Menkaure Pyramid to be 23gy. Remembering that the ratio of the gy scale to the gx scale is 0.733:1 and that the ratio of the gy scale to the gz scale is 1:1, I determined that the coordinates for the galactic body represented by the Menkaure Pyramid is (-0.733, 23, 23). The distance due north from the center of the easternmost Menkaure subsidiary pyramid to the center of the Khufu Pyramid is 192 gy and the coordinates for the galactic body represented by the Khufu Pyramid are (101.154, 192, 192).

Using these coordinates in space (Plate 8-2), I built four tri- angles to compare the position of the Menkaure Pyramid and the galactic body it represents

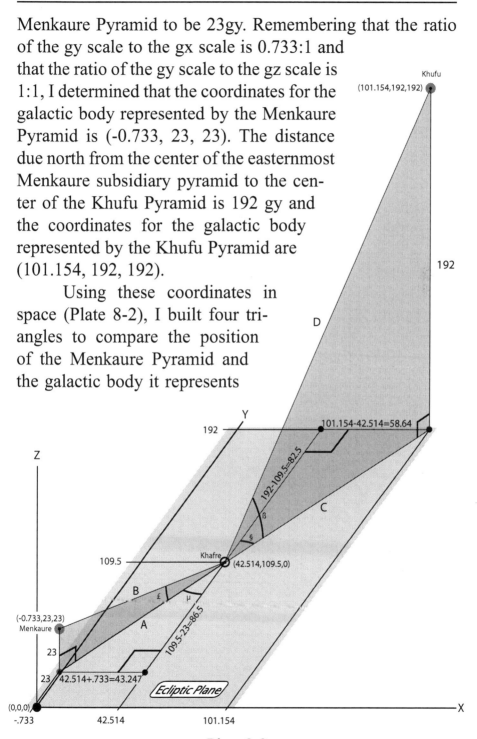

Plate 8-2

to the Khafre Pyramid, which represents the sun in our so-lar system; and the position of the Khufu Pyramid, and the galactic body it represents, to the Khafre Pyramid. First, I examined the two-dimensional triangle formed by the coordinates of the body represented by the Menkaure Pyramid. (See Plate 8-2a) I evaluated the distance from the center of the base of the Menkaure Pyramid to the center of the base of the Khafre Pyramid (line A) to be 96.709 units. I used trigonometry to determine the angle by which line A deviates westward from a true north to south line that passes through the center of the Khafre Pyramid, and that angle is 26.564 degrees. To my amazement, this is within ninety- one ten-thousandths of a degree, or 32.76 seconds of arc, of the measurement Lehner gives for the angle of descent (26.5731 degrees) of the descending passage in the Khufu Pyramid.

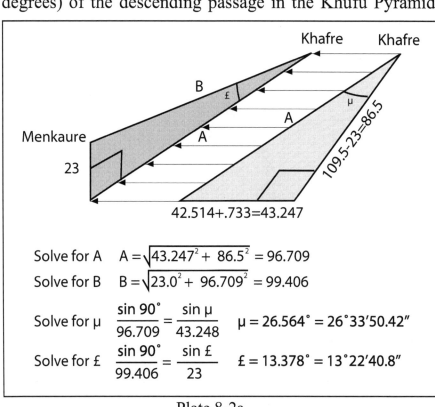

Plate 8-2a

[The descending passage is 191 feet and 11 inches long, according to Lehner, and its angle and orientation only deviate by less than one centimeter. Such precision must have been created to be used as a measurement tool.] Then, I examined the two-dimensional triangle formed with the z-coordinate perpendicular to the ecliptic plane and which shares line A. I used the Pythagorean Theorem to calculate the length of line B to be 99.406 units. Then, I used trigonometry to calculate the angle at which line B leaves, and deviates from, the ecliptic plane from our sun to the body represented by the apex of the Menkaure Pyramid to be 13.378 degrees.

Next, I examined the two-dimensional triangle formed by the coordinates of the bodies represented by the Khufu Pyramid and the Khafre Pyramid. (See Plate 8-2b) I evaluated the distance from the center of the base of the Khufu Pyramid to the center of the base of the Khafre Pyramid (line C) to be 101.217 units. I used trigonometry to determine the angle by which line C deviates eastward from a true north to south line that passes through the center of the Khafre Pyramid, and that angle is 35.404 degrees. Then, I examined the two-dimensional triangle formed with the z-coordinate perpendicular to the ecliptic plane and which shares line C. I used the Pythagorean Theorem to calculate the length of line D to be 217.046 units. Then, I used trigonometry to calculate the angle at which line D leaves, and deviates from, the ecliptic plane from our sun to the body represented by the apex of the Khufu Pyramid to be 62.203 degrees. I subtracted 62.203 degrees from 90 degrees to result in a complementary angle of 27.797 degrees. This angle is within 1.224 degrees of the Khufu descending passage angle. Because of the difference between the two angles, I realized that the lateral position, with reference to its deviation from the north to south line, of the point in space I am seeking must be calculated

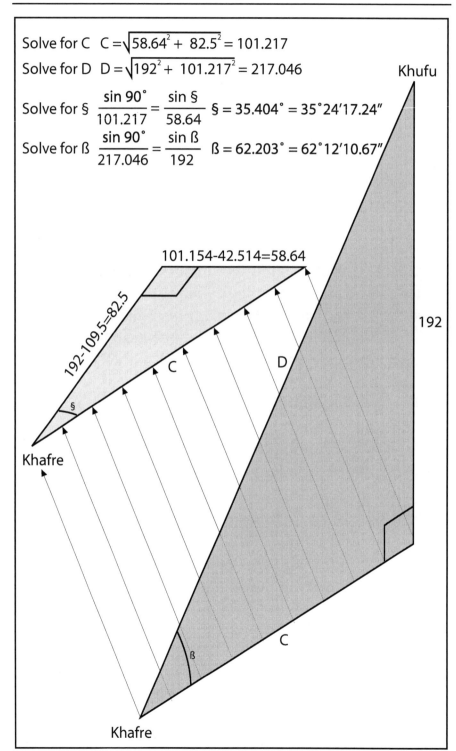

Solve for C $C = \sqrt{58.64^2 + 82.5^2} = 101.217$

Solve for D $D = \sqrt{192^2 + 101.217^2} = 217.046$

Solve for § $\dfrac{\sin 90°}{101.217} = \dfrac{\sin §}{58.64}$ § = 35.404° = 35°24′17.24″

Solve for ß $\dfrac{\sin 90°}{217.046} = \dfrac{\sin ß}{192}$ ß = 62.203° = 62°12′10.67″

Khufu

101.154-42.514=58.64

192-109.5=82.5

192

C

D

§

Khafre

ß

C

Khafre

Plate 8-2b

mathematically. I had expected the altitude I was seeking to be equivalent to the Khufu descending passage angle of 26.5731 degrees. Now, I realized that the altitude must be 90 degrees minus the Khufu descending passage angle which equals 63.4269 degrees.

[I will soon tell you what galactic body I have determined that the Khufu Pyramid, or Great Pyramid, represents. But, first, I had to determine the galactic body that the Menkaure Pyramid represents.]

Because I believe that the Menkaure Pyramid is a very significant element in the Giza pyramid complex, I put much energy into investigating what it represents. In the midst of my investigation one day, I turned on my laptop to begin my work. I must have shut down my laptop with the Starry Night Pro program on the last time I had used it because, to

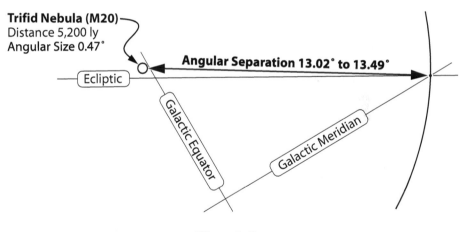

Plate 8-3

my delight, the Trifid Nebula (M-20) was right there in the middle of my screen. Out of curiosity, I dragged my curser over it and noted that the Trifid Nebula is located approximately 5,200 light years from our solar system and at a point near the intersection of the Milky Way galactic plane and the ecliptic plane. (Plate 8-3.) So, using the angular distance of

13.378 degrees, I drew a circle with that radius (13.378 degrees) centered on the Trifid Nebula and found that it intersected the ecliptic plane at the same point where the Galactic Meridian intersects the ecliptic plane. To be completely accurate, the Trifid Nebula is so huge that the angle between any point in the Trifid Nebula and the intersection of the ecliptic

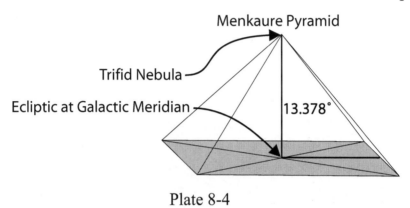

Plate 8-4

plane and the Galactic Meridian has a range of 13.02 degrees to 13.49 degrees. Hence, I could deduce that, the angle between a certain point within the Trifid Nebula and the intersection point of the Galactic Meridian with the ecliptic plane is precisely 13.378 degrees. (Plate 8-4) (Coincidentally, the angular size of the moon as viewed from Earth is the same: about one half of a degree.)

Remembering that the Giza pyramid complex had provided a secondary check for any solutions I had already discovered, I searched for that secondary check. Where else did I get a result of 5,200? I got a solution of 5,200.83 when I compared the angle of ascent to the top of the Khufu Pyramid to the angle of ascent to the top of the Menkaure Pyramid (using the conical transformation process introduced in Chapter 7 and described in Appendix B). I subtracted the smaller angle from the larger angle to get 0 degrees, 0 minutes, 39.66 seconds; then, I solved for the length of the base of a right triangle with that angle measurement at the opposite end of the 90 degree angle (see Plate 8-5). Hence, all of this indicates that the Trifid Nebula is the body referenced by the Menkaure Pyramid!

Menkaure Pyramid Adjusted to Square Base

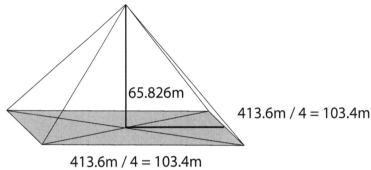

65.826m

413.6m / 4 = 103.4m

413.6m / 4 = 103.4m

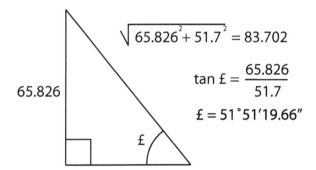

$$\sqrt{65.826^2 + 51.7^2} = 83.702$$

$$\tan £ = \frac{65.826}{51.7}$$

$$£ = 51°51'19.66''$$

65.826

103.4 / 2 = 51.7

Menkaure = 51°51'19.66"
Khufu = 51°50'40"
_____
0°0'39.66"

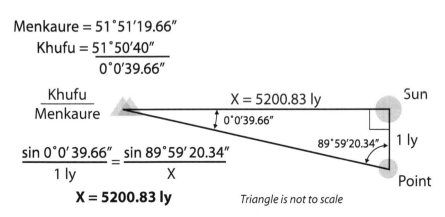

Khufu
_____
Menkaure

X = 5200.83 ly   Sun

0°0'39.66"

89°59'20.34"   1 ly

$$\frac{\sin 0°0'39.66''}{1\ ly} = \frac{\sin 89°59'20.34''}{X}$$

X = 5200.83 ly

Point

Triangle is not to scale

Plate 8-5

The Trifid Nebula has three very interesting characteristics which have been observed through telescopes in addition to having the same angular range as the moon. "Trifid" means "three lobes," referring to its appearance. It is an emission nebula, which means that it contains about 3,100 forming stars that ionize gases and cause them to glow red. (The base of the Menkaure Pyramid, to 16 courses up, is made of unpolished red granite- a solid material, and yet not polished. Could this be a coincidence, or is this confirmation that the Menkaure Pyramid represents the Trifid Nebula?) It is also a reflection nebula which means that the dust particles within the nebula are scattered appropriately to catch and reflect the light emitted from the forming stars. Thirdly, it is a dark nebula because it also contains gases that are so dense that they obscure any light from passing through them. (The sarcophagus that had been removed and lost in a shipwreck was reported to have been made of a dark material.) The net effect is visually impressive. The Trifid Nebula is a veritable nursery for baby stars, while other nebulae are rest homes for dying stars. So, the Trifid Nebula is a very important, and positive, part of our galaxy.

So, what galactic body does the Great Khufu Pyramid represent? Of the three pyramids, it is the largest yet does not contain any granite on its exterior surface. In my opinion, this indicates that it does not represent, or contain, anything solid. It is slightly skewed from a north to south alignment by 3 minutes and 6 seconds. This misalignment eluded me for some time, but I eventually discovered its significance. Using the Galactic Meridian, referenced by the Menkaure Pyramid, as my reference point and our point on the ecliptic plane, represented by the Khafre Pyramid, I could now determine the coordinate location of what is represented by the Khufu Pyramid. (Conventional astronomy uses the northern hemisphere vernal equinox as its primary referential direction in the Celestial coordinate system, which changes with precession. However, using the point where the Galactic Meridian intersects the ecliptic as a primary referential point is superior as the relative angles to points in the galaxy do not change.)

I noticed that the angle of ascent from our point represented by the Khafre Pyramid on the ecliptic plane to the point represented by the apex of the Khufu Pyramid above the ecliptic plane (where the z-coordinate equals the y-coordinate) is approximately equal to 90 degrees minus the angle of the descending passage, but off by nearly one degree. Hence, I realized that the descending passage angle is significant, but a more accurate calculation needed to be used to solve this part of the Giza pyramid complex galactic map. Using the angle of 90 degrees minus the Khufu Pyramid descending passage angle, I created a graph of all of the x-y coordinates, where z=y and the angle to the point, with the coordinate (x, y, z), from the Khafre Pyramid (where y=109.5) is maintained at 90 degrees minus the Khufu descending passage angle. (See Plate 8-6) Then, I increased the y-value by 10 unit increments and solved for the corresponding x-values. When the solutions were plotted on a graph, I saw that a perpendicular vertical line drawn from the initial solution point on the x-axis (where y=109.5) intersected my curve of solutions at a point approximately 73 units above the x-axis. (Remember that there are 73 evenly spaced workmen's barracks running vertically and parallel to the Peribolus Wall.) So, it occurred to me that this intersection point on the curve of solutions must be significant.

I plugged the exact x-value for the base of the point of intersection (which is 54.77 units) and solved for the exact vertical distance (which is 73.06996 units) to the exact point

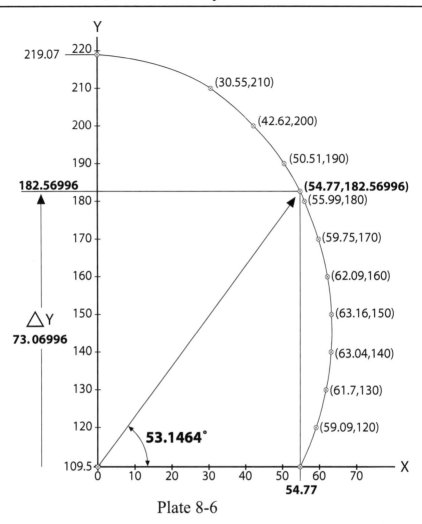

Plate 8-6

of intersection. The x-y coordinates of that point are (54.77, 182.56996). Now, I could solve for the angle from the x-axis to the point of intersection, which I found to be 53.1464 degrees. I added the descending passage angle (26.5731 degrees) and added 90 degrees and added 53.1464 degrees for a total of 169.7195 degrees. (See Plate 8-7) This result indicates how far around the ecliptic plane the target point is from the intersection of the Galactic Meridian and the ecliptic plane. Lastly, I determined, by subtracting the descending passage angle from 90 degrees, that the solution point is lo-

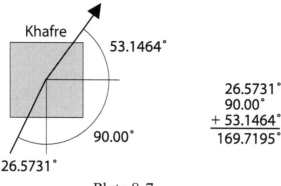

Plate 8-7

cated 63.4269 degrees above the ecliptic plane. So, now we know exactly where the direction in the galaxy represented by the Khufu Pyramid is located.

Using the ecliptic plane and the Galactic Meridian as my guides, I marked out where the two intersect at a specific date and time (J2000: January 1, 2000 at 11:58:55 UTC, or 3:58:55 am PST). [From this point on, I will substitute longitudinal and latitudinal terms of "minutes" and seconds" for decimal amounts. This is the standard for dealing with the ecliptic coordinate system.] They intersected on the ecliptic at two points: at approximately 77 degrees, 20 minutes and 23.25 seconds and at 257 degrees, 20 minutes and 23.25 seconds. I used the latter position because it is located approximately 13 degrees from the Trifid Nebula (Plate 8-8). Then, I added 169 degrees, 43 minutes and 10.2 seconds to this position to arrive at the position of 67 degrees, 3 minutes and 33.29 seconds. Finally, I moved the position into the third dimension (altitude) by 63 degrees, 25 minutes and 37 seconds (90 degrees minus the descending passage angle). The resulting position is located at the ecliptic longitude of 67 degrees, 3 minutes and 33.29 seconds and the ecliptic latitude of 63 degrees, 25 minutes and 37 seconds. (Plate 8-9)

When I looked on a star map in this part of the

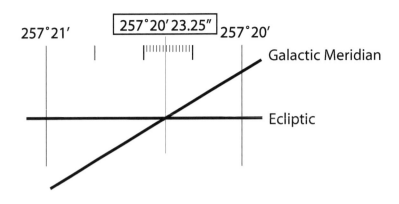

257°21'   257°20' 23.25"   257°20'

Galactic Meridian

Ecliptic

J2000: 01/01/2000 11:58:55 UTC (3:58:55AM Pacific Time)

Plate 8-8

Milky Way Galaxy, I saw a group of eight stars (seven of which are arranged in an elliptical system with one in the approximate center): USNO J0028514+795232, USNO J0028170+795228, USNO J0029168+795053, USNO J0029060+794822, USNO J0027564+794809, USNO J0028317+794600, USNO J0027487+794429, and USNO J0026506+794412.

There are two other stars indicated by my computations. They are USNO J0030020+794901 (which is far off the ellipse) and HIP 2299 (which is closer to the ellipse defined by the eight stars being 1,591 light years away from Earth; and hence, is much "brighter" with an apparent magnitude of 10.46 and three times the size of our sun). Although I believe that these two stars are also significant, I have been focusing on the eight stars because they are located in an elliptical pattern and their magnitudes (brightness from Earth's perspective) are close to one another with apparent magnitudes ranging from 12.85 to 14.45.

In 2013, the satellite Gaia was launched by the European Space Agency with the purpose of creating a three dimensional map of our galaxy. As of this date, although the

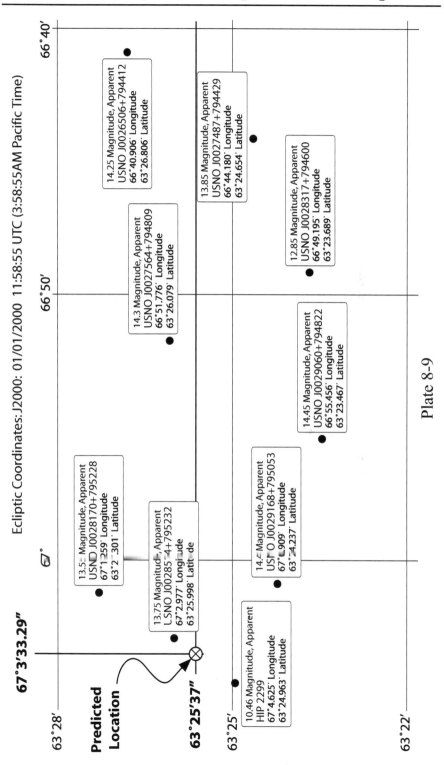

Ecliptic Coordinates:J2000: 01/01/2000 11:58:55 UTC (3:58:55AM Pacific Time)

67°3'33.29"

Predicted Location

63°25'37"

14.25 Magnitude, Apparent
USNO J0026506+794412
66°40.906' Longitude
63°26.806' Latitude

13.85 Magnitude, Apparent
USNO J0027487+794429
66°44.180' Longitude
63°24.654' Latitude

14.3 Magnitude, Apparent
USNO J0027564+794809
66°51.776' Longitude
63°26.079' Latitude

12.85 Magnitude, Apparent
USNO J0028317+794600
66°49.195' Longitude
63°23.689' Latitude

14.45 Magnitude, Apparent
USNO J0029060+794822
66°55.456' Longitude
63°23.467' Latitude

13.5 Magnitude, Apparent
USNO J0028170+795228
67°1.259' Longitude
63°27.301' Latitude

13.75 Magnitude, Apparent
USNO J0028574+795232
67°2.977' Longitude
63°25.998' Latitude

14.4 Magnitude, Apparent
USNO J0029168+795053
67°0.909' Longitude
63°24.237' Latitude

10.46 Magnitude, Apparent
HIP 2299
67°4.625' Longitude
63°24.963' Latitude

Plate 8-9

data became available in 2018, I have not figured out how to cross-reference their data with that on my Starry Night Pro program. Before the 2013 launch, I began a set of calculations in order to answer my question myself. I noticed that, if an imaginary line were extended toward the workmen's barracks from the causeways leading from the Khufu Pyramid and Khafre Pyramid, the lines would intersect at the 31st barrack from the center barrack. A circle with a radius of 31 Giza y-units and drawn concentrically with the center of the Khafre Pyramid circumscribes the pyramid and passes through the subsidiary pyramid to the south of the pyramid. This was significant to me because the average radius of our solar system equals approximately 31 astronomical units. Thus, I measured the angle from an imaginary line perpendicular to the barrack to each of the causeways and discovered that they were congruent at 15 degrees each and totaled 30 degrees. However, because these two angles are congruent and reflect off the perpendicular line, I deduced that they do not represent distance, but do represent time. Using the astronomical precession cycle of Earth (25,771.5 years), I divided by 360 degrees to calculate that it takes 71.59 years for Earth to precess one degree and 2,147.7 years to process 30 degrees. So, the distance to this system from Earth is 2,147.7 light years.

What is the significance of this elliptical system I was directed to by the galactic map embedded in the Giza pyramid complex? Please read on.

Chapter 9

The Eight Stars of the 73 Cairn System

My next curiosity to be solved was whether any of the eight stars is similar to our Sun. To answer this question, I needed to know the distance of each of the eight stars from our Sun, which we solved for in the last chapter. When I applied the distance of 2,147.7 light years to each of the eight stars in the elliptical system, I was able to calculate their absolute magnitudes.

The apparent magnitude of an object is its brightness to the observer. The apparent magnitude scale was created by Hipparchus, a Greek astronomer and mathematician. From the perspective of a human on Earth, our Sun has an apparent magnitude of -27 because it is so close to us. The smaller the apparent magnitude, the brighter the object appears to the observer. The faintest star that can be observed by the average human eye has an apparent magnitude of +6. To see a dimmer star with a larger apparent magnitude, the observer must use a telescope. Whereas a star with an apparent magnitude of +1 is 100 times brighter than a star with an apparent magnitude of +6; a star with an apparent magnitude of +11 is 100 times dimmer than a star with an apparent magnitude of +6. The eight stars identified by the Giza pyramid complex have apparent magnitudes that range from +12.85 to +14.45. In other words, they are not visible to the human eye. In fact, it would take a powerful telescope (not invented until the late 1700s AD) to see these stars which are from 549 to 2,399 times dimmer than what you can see without one.

In order to compare our Sun to other stars, we must use a magnitude comparison tool that was created in 1856 by Norman Pogson. The comparison value is calculated by taking the fifth root of 100 (approximately 2.512 and called Pogson's Ratio) and raise that to the power of the difference between the apparent magnitudes of the two stars being compared. This is how I was able to determine the comparable dimness of the eight stars.

To find the absolute magnitude of a star, you must use the distance modulus formula based on parsecs (which was a distance unit created by Herbert Hall Turner in 1913). The distance modulus formula is M = m-5(log base 10[distance in light years/light years per parsec] - 1), where m is the apparent magnitude, and M is the absolute magnitude. After all of my calculations, I discovered that seven of the eight stars in this elliptical system are approximately the same absolute magnitude (4.46 to 5.36) as our Sun (which has an absolute magnitude of 4.83) and seven of the eight would be considered solar type stars. The eighth star has an absolute magnitude of 3.76; however, when I included the absolute magnitude of the eighth star in a calculation of the average absolute magnitude of all eight stars, the result was 4.83: the absolute magnitude of our Sun! (Plate 9-1)

2148 Light Years

Star Name	Apparent (m)	Absolute (M)
USNO J0028170+795228	13.55	4.46
USNO J0028514+795232	13.75	4.66
USNO J0029168+795053	14.40	5.31
USNO J0029060+794822	14.45	5.36
USNO J0028317+794600	12.85	3.76
USNO J0027487+794429	13.85	4.76
USNO J0026506+794412	14.25	5.16
USNO J0027564+794809	14.30	5.21

$$M = m - 5\left(\log_{10} \frac{d/ly}{ly/parsec} - 1\right)$$

$$M = m - 5\left(\log_{10} \frac{2148}{3.26156} - 1\right)$$

$$M = m - 9.093$$

For Absolute (M)
$n = 8$
$\Sigma x = 38.66$
$\bar{x} = 4.83$ (*SUN = 4.83*)
$\sigma_n = 0.50990195$

Plate 9-1

Around 1910, a scatter plot diagram comparing the absolute magnitude, effective temperature, luminosity, and spectral class of different types of stars was created by Ejnar Hertzsprung and Henry Norris Russell. This is called the Hertzsprung-Russell Diagram, or H-R Diagram, or HRD (Plate 9-2). Our Sun is a star in the Main Sequence classification with a luminosity of 1, an absolute magnitude of 4.83, a temperature of 5,778 Kelvin, and spectral class G2V. Although I was unable to find the effective temperature and spectral class of the eight stars I am referring to, I do know their absolute magnitudes and luminosities, and I know that they are within the Main Sequence classification. By plotting their known qualities onto the H-R diagram, I can know their probable effective temperatures and spectral classes. (Plate 9-3)

A solar type star has a spectral class within the range from F8V through K2V, and this definition applies to approximately 10% of all stars. A more narrow definition of a

Hertzsprung-Russell Diagram & "Stars of 73 Cairn System" With Main Sequence Position

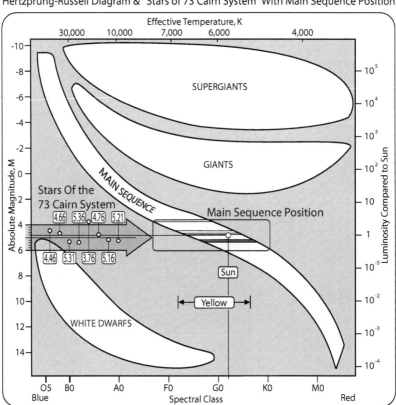

Plate 9-2

solar type star is a solar analog, which measures the metallicity and effective temperature of a star; and evaluates whether or not it has a companion with an orbital period of ten days or less. Metallicity is the abundance of elements present in a star that are heavier than hydrogen and helium (which would be necessary for planet formation). And a star companion with an orbital period of ten days or less would stimulate stellar activity. An even more narrow definition of a solar type star is called a solar twin. A solar twin to our Sun would be a G2V star with a surface temperature of 5,778 Kelvin; it would be 4.6 billion years old with a correct metallicity, and a luminosity variation of 0.1%. To date, the solar twin to our Sun has not been located.

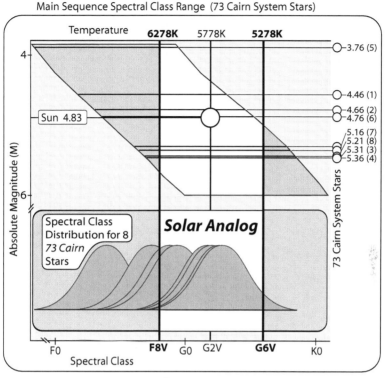

Main Sequence Spectral Class Range (73 Cairn System Stars)

Plate 9-3

If you look at Plate 9-3, you can see that six, or seven, of the eight stars in the group fall into the range of the solar analog within the main sequence spectral class range. The spectral class of a star indicates the age of a star and its effective temperature. The spectral class of a star also indicates the presence of certain metals (metallicity) within the star and the luminosity, or absolute magnitude, of the star. These six, or seven, stars have a probability of supporting an inhabitable planet. Of the six, or seven, stars within the solar analog range, one star (USNO J0027487+794429, with an absolute magnitude of 4.76) is very close in luminosity to our Sun, with an absolute magnitude of 4.83. However, four of the stars within the solar analog range (USNO J0026506+794412, with an absolute magnitude of 5.16; USNO J0027564+794809, with an absolute magnitude of

5.21; USNO J0029168+795053, with an absolute magnitude of 5.31; and USNO J0029060+794822, with an absolute magnitude of 5.36) may be more stable stars and better candidates for supporting a planet with life. (Plate 9-4)

Thus, the Giza pyramid complex may be a galactic map pointing to similar solar type systems, each with a planet that may be inhabitable by Earthlings at some time. Could

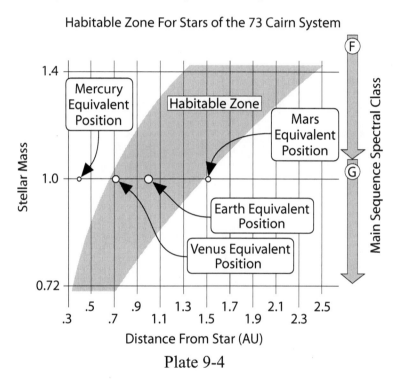

Plate 9-4

the Giza pyramid complex be a map pointing to alternate Earths? Could the Giza pyramid complex be a map pointing to Heaven?

Chapter 10

Verifying the Oval Solution

When the eight stars are plotted in their locations, the resulting configuration is an oval comprising seven stars with the eighth star in the middle (Plate 10-1). The oval of

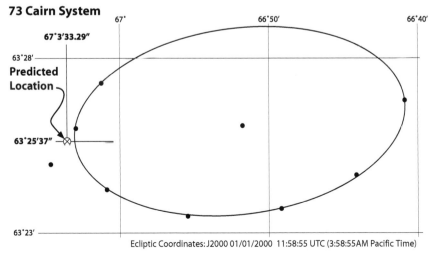

Plate 10-1

stars in my solution is pointed to by the constellation Cepheus, "King" (Plate 10-2). Cepheus was an Ethiopian king in Greek mythology and included in the poems, *The Iliad* and *The Odyssey* by Homer. The constellation Cepheus was listed by the 2nd Century astronomer Ptolemy. I drew a horizontal line through the center of the oval to create a semi-major axis, and I drew a vertical line through the center of the oval to create a semi-minor axis (Plate 10-3). I noticed that

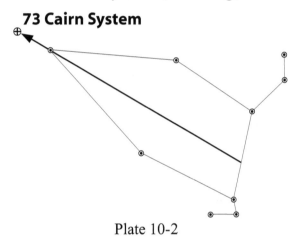

Plate 10-2

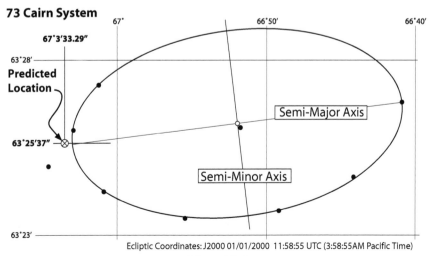

Plate 10-3

the center star is located very close to the intersection point of the semi-major and semi-minor axes. And the solution point, with the latitude of 63 degrees, 25minutes, 37seconds,

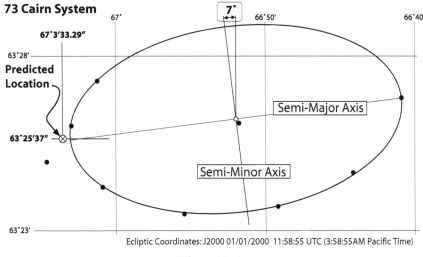

Plate 10-4

is situated very near the intersection of the semi-major axis and the oval. Also, note that the oval configuration is canted by 7 degrees off the ecliptic plane (Plate 10-4).

Next, I scaled the oval configuration to overlay the Giza pyramid complex such that the intersection point of the semi-major and semi-minor axes did lie on the center of the Khafre Pyramid, and the oval as well as the 7 degree deviation line from the semi-minor axis ran through the center of the Khufu Pyramid (Plate 10-5). When I rotated the oval 7 degrees (to match the degree to which the oval star system is canted off the ecliptic plane), I saw that the semi-major axis passes through the corner of the workmen's barracks in one direction and the Menkaure causeway termination in the opposite direction (Plate 10-6). Moreover, the ecliptic latitude line of 63 degrees, 25minutes, 37seconds, on which the solution point lies, runs through the center of the

73 Cairn System Giza Site Overlays

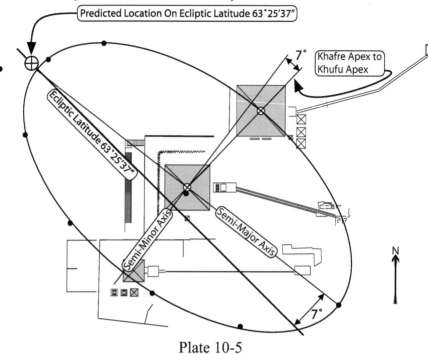

Plate 10-5

Plate 10-6

73 Cairn System Giza Site Overlay

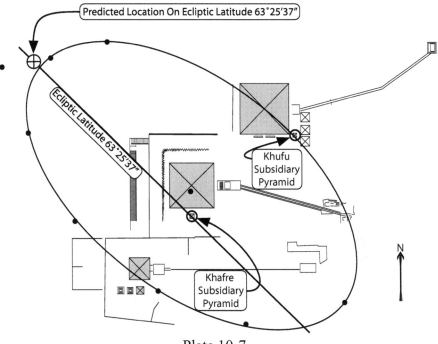

Plate 10-7

Khafre subsidiary pyramid; while the oval passes through the Khufu subsidiary pyramid (Plate 10-7). Additionally, the star USNO J0028170+795228 lines up with the temple at the east end of the Khufu Pyramid causeway and the star USNO J0027487+794429 lines up with the termination point of the southernmost Menkaure Pyramid enclosure wall. (Plate 10-8) In Plate 10-9, you can see that an extension northward of the enclosure wall to the immediate west of the Menkaure Pyramid runs through star USNO J0028170+795228. Also, in Plate 10-9, you can see that an extension of the northward branch (before the bend) of the southernmost Menkaure Pyramid enclosure runs through star USNO J0028317+794600, which also lines up with the centers of the three Menkaure Queens' Pyramids. [This star happens to have the greatest apparent magnitude.]

Then, I drew a northward line through the center of

73 Cairn System Giza Site Overlays

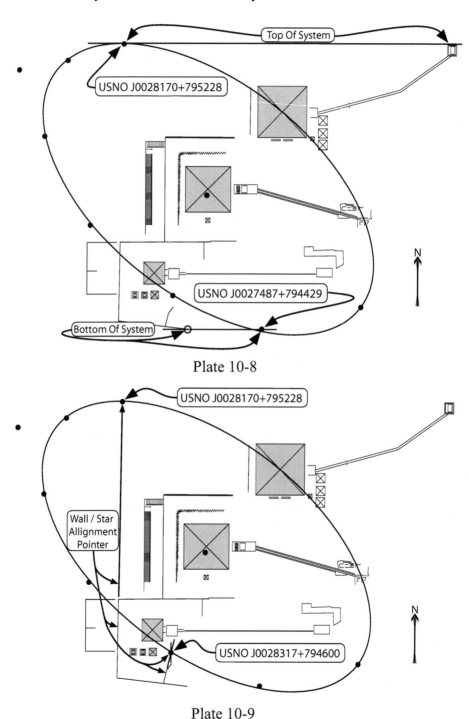

Plate 10-8

Plate 10-9

73 Cairn System Giza Site Overlay

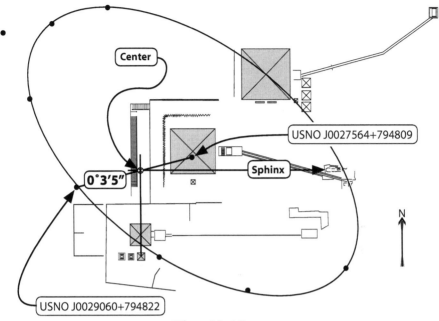

Plate 10-10

the eastern Menkaure Queen's Pyramid (which I have designated as the reference point from which I drew the three-dimensional map in the chapter, "The Giza Pyramid Complex Galactic Map"); and I drew a line from the center star USNO J0027564+794809 within the oval to the fourth, or center, star on the oval USNO J0029060+794822. (Plate 10-10) A line drawn to the east, from the intersection point, runs directly toward the Sphinx and through the Sphinx Temple. [In the chapter titled, "Design of the Giza Pyramid Complex", I stated that the Sphinx is oriented such that it appears to be greeting the sunrise or guarding the complex. Curiously, the Sphinx appears to be guarding the oval star system as well.] I also noted that the angular distance between the center star within the oval and the fourth (central) star along the oval is 3 minutes, 5 seconds (within 1 second of the misalignment of the Khufu Pyramid from a true cardinal orientation).

Khufu Pyramid

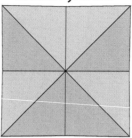

Plate 10-11

There is even more evidence that the Khufu Pyramid represents the oval star system in the Giza pyramid complex galactic map. The Khufu Pyramid (representing the eight stars of the oval star system) has eight faces of what used to be polished limestone. (Plate 10-11) "But, a pyramid has four faces," you might say. This is typically true. However, upon examination of the Khufu Pyramid from above during the Equinox, one can clearly see that each of the four sides of the pyramid is indented at the center. Thus, the Khufu Pyramid actually has eight faces.

One more reference to the eight stars of the system is found within the Grand Gallery that ascends within the Khufu Pyramid. In Piazzi Smyth's book titled, *Our Inheritance In the Great Pyramid*, published in 1874, the Grand Gallery (Plate 10-12 and Plate 10-13) which connects the entrance to the Queen's Chamber passage to the entrance to the King's Chamber passage, ascends at approximately the same angle as

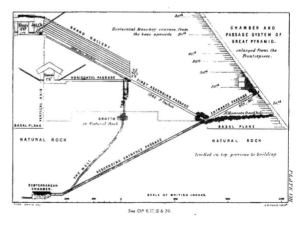

Plate 10-12

the descending passage (26 degrees, 34 minutes, 23 seconds) and has eight faces. Additionally in Plate 10-13, it is apparent that, unlike the other seven faces, the fifth face from the top has a groove cut into the face that runs the length of the Grand Gallery. There are four faces above the grooved face and three faces below it. Could it be that this grooved face is a reference to the central star on the oval (Plate 10-10) which has four stars above it and three stars below?

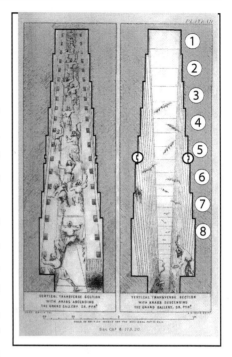

Plate 10-13

Thirty years of examination of the Giza pyramid complex have culminated in my hypothesis that the complex is a galactic map pointing to an oval star system comprised of eight stars. And this oval star system contains at least one excellent candidate for a solar system that may have an inhabitable planet orbiting its sun. There is probably more evidence embedded within the Giza pyramid complex. As I have stated before, I believe that each element in the complex is significant. Nothing in the complex was put there by accident. Nonetheless, I have not discovered the significance of every element yet. I leave some discoveries for you to make, if you are so inclined.

So, now that I have scientifically deciphered the Giza pyramid complex for you, please indulge me as I relay what I believe is the future purpose of the information the Giza pyramid complex provides humankind.

Hannah Anderson

Chapter 11

The Giza Pyramid Complex: Word of God

Piazzi Smyth wrote in the Preface to his book, *Our Inheritance In The Great Pyramid*:

And although some well-meaning persons may have too hastily concluded, merely because they do not find the very name of Pyramid written down in Scripture, that therefore there is nothing about the Great Pyramid in the Bible, -yet they may rest perfectly assured that there is a great deal about the Bible subject, in the Great Pyramid. Which building is moreover an earlier document in the history of the human race; while the putting together of its stones into the vocal and deeply-meaning shapes we see them in now, was absolutely contemporary with the first of the primeval events to which it was destined to bear indubitable witness in these latter days, and not sooner.

And, as introduction to the Preface, Smyth quoted from the

Bible book of Jeremiah 32:20: "You have set signs and wonders in the land of Egypt, to this day..." Although Piazzi Smyth recognized God's part in the construction of the Great Pyramid, he did not justify his hypothesis. Perhaps he, too, wanted to pique interest in others to follow through with proving the connection between God and the Great Pyramid he so meticulously measured.

As I relayed in the Foreward and in other chapters in this book, I also believe that the Giza pyramid complex was built with guidance from God and contains a time specific message within its carefully created design. However, the embedded message could not, and cannot be, deciphered and explained without widespread distribution of the Bible (containing the Old and New Testaments), relatively new astronomical formulae and recently invented tools, and a developing interdisciplinary mindset to encourage the exchange of ideas between disciplines.

Widespread Distribution of the Bible

Human beings have been given many opportunities and challenges throughout their existence with the Word of God most readily available to all only after the widespread imitation of Gutenberg's revolutionary block typeset publishing technique. Once the mass production of the Bible, at an affordable price, and the expansion of the existence of loaning libraries throughout the world were commonplace, most humans had access to God's Word. However, this is a phenomenon accomplished less than 600 years ago. In comparison, the Giza pyramid complex was constructed thousands of years ago, perhaps soon after the creation of human beings. Because the Giza pyramid complex was constructed long before the birth of the authors of the Bible, with the

Great Flood dividing the history of human beings, I believe that the connection between the Bible and the Giza pyramid complex has rarely been recognized. I believe that now is the time God intended for us to recognize the connection.

Biblical Reference to Egypt

Before I explain how the Bible directs attention to the Giza pyramid complex, I must point out how the Bible directs to Egypt. We know that Egypt is significant to the history, and the future, of humankind because the Bible directs our focus to the significance of Egypt in the Book of Isaiah numerous times. In Isaiah 19:1, we read, "Behold, the Lord is riding on a swift cloud and is coming into Egypt". And, when God sent his only son to us, Jesus' parents sought refuge in Egypt to protect Jesus from death, as we read in Matthew 2:13-15:

> Now when they [the Magi] departed, behold, an angel of the Lord appeared to Joseph in a dream, saying, "Arise, take the young Child and His mother, flee to Egypt, and stay there until I bring you word; for Herod will seek the young Child to destroy Him."
>
> When he arose, he took the young Child and His mother by night and departed for Egypt, and was there until the death of Herod, that it might be fulfilled which was spoken by the Lord through the prophet, saying, "Out of Egypt I called My Son."

And, continued in Matthew 2:19-21:

> But when Herod was dead, behold, an angel of the Lord appeared in a dream to Joseph in Egypt, saying, "Arise, take the young Child and His mother, and go to the land of Israel, for those who sought the young Child's life are dead."
>
> Then he arose, took the young Child and His

mother, and came into the land of Israel.

In reference to more recent history, I discovered in Is
iah 19:18-25:

> In that day there will be five cities in the land
> of Egypt speaking language of Ca'naan and swearing
> loyalty to Jehovah of armies. One city will be called
> The City of Tearing Down.
> In that day there will be an altar to Jehovah in
> the middle of the land of Egypt and a pillar to Jehovah
> at its boundary. It will be for a sign and for a witness
> to Jehovah of armies in the land of Egypt; for they will
> cry out to Jehovah because of the oppressors, and he
> will send them a savior, a grand one, who will save
> them. And Jehovah will become known to the Egyp-
> tians, and the Egyptians will know Jehovah in that
> day, and they will offer sacrifices and gifts to make a
> vow to Jehovah and pay it. Jehovah will strike Egypt,
> striking and healing it; and they will return to Jehovah,
> and he will respond to their entreaties and heal them.
> In that day there will be a highway out of Egypt
> to Assyria. Then Assyria will come into Egypt, and
> Egypt into Assyria, and Egypt will serve God together
> with Assyria. In that day Israel will be the third along
> with Egypt and with Assyria, a blessing in the midst of
> the earth, whom the Lord of hosts has blessed, saying,
> "Blessed be Egypt my people, and Assyria the work of
> my hands, and Israel my inheritance."

If you examine a map of Egypt, you will find a curved
chain of five oases which took 40 days to traverse by cara-
van. The southernmost oasis, near the center of Egypt, is
called the Kharga Oasis. Within the Kharga Oasis is El Baga-
wat, an ancient Christian cemetery which was used from 300
to 700 AD and is the best preserved of all ancient Christian

cemeteries. At the center of the five oases is Asyut. The modern city of Asyut is home to one of the largest Coptic Catholic churches in Egypt. The Coptic name of the city is Syowt, which means "Guardian" of the northern approach of Upper Egypt. A distinct dialect of Coptic, "Lycopolitan," was spoken there during Greco-Roman times. Asyut is located at the end of a 40 Day Road that connected the city to Darfur, Sudan through the Selima and Kharga Oases. Coptic Christians originated in Northern Africa, primarily Libya, Sudan, and Egypt. Approximately half of the residents of Modern Asyut are Coptic Christian. On August 17, 2000, the Virgin Mary is reported to have appeared in Asyut. I believe that this curved chain of five oases, with the city of Asyut at its center, is the scenario prophesied by Isaiah and indicates that other prophesies may be coming to fruition.

I believe, in line with past examiners of elements of the Giza pyramid complex, that clues to our origins and our future are embedded within the Giza pyramid complex. Piazzi Smyth, whom I quoted at the beginning of this chapter, adopted the idea that the Great Pyramid was constructed under the direction of God from John Taylor, who wrote *The Great Pyramid, Why It Was Built and Who Built It* in 1859. Taylor believed that the Great Pyramid was planned by Noah, who had supervised its construction. Taylor also believed that the concept of pi and the golden ration were deliberately incorporated into its design. Smyth, an astronomer, believed that the Great Pyramid was a repository of prophesies which could be revealed by detailed measurement of the structure. Charles Russell, who owned a chain of five clothing stores, became a minister and founded the religious Bible Students Movement, which was named Jehovah's Witnesses in 1931 by his successor, Joseph F. Rutherford. Smyth's prophesies regarding the Great Pyramid were integrated into certain prophesies by

Russell which adopted Smyth's prediction regarding the date of the second coming of Christ. After Charles Russell's passing in 1916, Rutherford denounced pyramidology as being unscriptural. However, about half of Russell's followers did not follow Rutherford, and a percentage of them continued to practice pyramidology. I would be very interested in having a discussion with any descendants of said group.

Modern Tools

Some of the tools that were necessary to help us decipher the Giza pyramid complex, and what it represents, were invented relatively recently. During the past few hundred years, those tools have been refined and are nearing perfection. Only 225 years ago, a telescope strong enough to see the ellipse of stars I have referred to was invented. And only 175 years ago, Pogson's ratio was introduced into the world of Astronomy to compare faraway stars. Within my lifetime, various tools and technologies have been invented that will aid in surveying the Giza pyramid complex and all of its elements. There are now drones that can help us look down from above. There are tiny robots that can be directed between walls, or through shafts, to collect video data; or even retrieve items for further analysis. There is ground penetrating radar that can help us "see" what lies beneath. And there are micro CT scans that can read delicate, ancient scrolls without unfurling them. In other words, what past Egyptologists accomplished with surveying equipment, dynamite, and bulldozers, we can now accomplish without damaging the elements within the Giza pyramid complex.

Interdisciplinary Mindset

The last tool necessary to decipher the Word of God embedded in the Giza pyramid complex is an interdisciplinary mindset and its widespread use. This has been developing during my lifetime, but has experienced setbacks recently, and was introduced by Jesus. In Matthew 13:10-16 we read:

>And the disciples came and said to Him, 'Why do You speak to them in parables?'
>
>He answered and said to them, "Because it has been given to you to know the mysteries of the kingdom of heaven, but to them it has not been given.
>
>For whatever has, to him more will be given, and he will have abundance; but whoever does not have, even what he has will be taken away from him.
>
>Therefore I speak to them in parables, because seeing they do not see, and hearing they do not hear, nor do they understand.
>
>And in them the prophecy of Isaiah is fulfilled, which says:
>'Hearing you will hear
>and shall not understand,
>And seeing you will see
>and not perceive;
>For the heart of this people
>has grown dull.
>Their ears are hard of hearing,
>And their eyes they have closed,
>Lest they should see with their eyes
>and hear with their ears,
>Lest they should understand
>with their heart and turn,
>So that I should heal them.'
>
>But blessed are your eyes for they see, and your ears for they hear; for assuredly, I say to you that

many prophets and righteous men desired to see what you see, and did not see it, and to hear what you hear, and did not hear it."

Recent Connections

To connect the dots between these Scriptures and the purpose of the Giza pyramid complex, I believe I had to experience the Covid-19 pandemic. During the pandemic, there were people who heard the science and saw victims in the hospital, yet they did not understand the significance of the pandemic. On the other hand, there were people who quickly understood the gravity of the situation, accepted scientific explanations and recommendations, and responded by taking responsibility for the health of others. They showed compassion and protected others from the virus in various ways, but they all understood in their hearts that they had to respond to the situation obediently, even though it might cost them personally, in the short term. They had to have faith that their efforts would result in a benefit for humankind in the long term. They understood.

The Covid-19 pandemic was a message from God. Jesus is not among us in body to explain it to us, but God's spirit is. In the same way, I believe the Giza pyramid complex was built to hold a message from God for the future of humankind. Once the message is fully deciphered, it will be readable by all humans, no matter their language, religion, discipline, or viewpoint because it is even more universal in interpretation than a parable: it is a three-dimensional cairn. It points the way to the answer. However, until humans adopt an interdisciplinary mindset and can exchange ideas between disciplines without judgment, the Truth cannot be revealed to all.

In John 3:11-12 we read:

> Jesus said to Nicodemus, a man of the Phari-
> sees and a ruler of the Jews, "Most assuredly, I say to
> you, 'We speak what We know and testify what We
> have seen, and you do not receive Our witness. If I
> have told you earthly things and you do not believe,
> how will you believe if I tell you heavenly things?'"

Hannah Anderson

Chapter 12

The Giza Pyramid Complex Revelation

I have long considered the Bible to be a manual for humans to refer to for guidance as to how to peacefully coexist, given all of our flaws. I have read other useful manuals relayed from God through highly receptive humans who tried to explain the truth of our existence and how to peacefully negotiate our individual paths while fellow human beings do the same. Some of the material found in other manuals were relayed hundreds of years before Christ walked the Earth (such as the Sutras relayed by the Buddha Siddhartha Gautama), and some were relayed hundreds of years after (such as the Koran relayed by Muhammad ibn Abdullah). I have great difficulty with the fact that these conveyances of God's Words from enlightened humans from different parts of the Earth with different racial, ethnic, and cultural backgrounds are perceived as different, when the core message to them all is the same. I honestly believe that human flaws have contributed to the grave mistake that many humans make when they believe that their way of honoring and serving God is the only true way to do so.

When God made it so that people could not understand each other's language so that they would disperse from Babel and populate the rest of the Earth, we are told that God did so because humans were trying to build a tower to Heaven. When I read about this part of human history, I realize that most humans have not learned nor changed their behavior since Adam and Eve succumbed to the desire to know all that God knows, the fatal flaw which Satan ignited in them and which cost us perfect, peaceful, and eternal life in the Garden of Eden. I believe God dispersed us so that He could know that, no matter how we honor and serve Him, we serve God because we want to honor and serve Him, and not because, or in the same way that others we are surrounded by do. I believe that this is the true meaning of the free will we are given by God.

My point here is that everything we have, and everything we are, are gifts from God. How we use each gift is dependent on how we use our free will to honor and serve God. God presented us with His Word through the Bible and other manuals and we, who choose to serve and honor God, use His manuals to learn how to coexist peacefully with other humans in preparation to be worthy of later coexisting with God, Christ, and the Celestial Beings in Heaven. That is the point to our existence after all, isn't it?

So, if God directed the construction of the Giza pyramid complex for us as a map, a computer, and a non-literary Book of Genesis, then I believe that the Book of Revelation is also embedded in the complex. The Alpha and the Omega; our beginning and our end must also be "written" in the design of the Giza pyramid complex. I haven't found it yet, but that does not mean it isn't there. Could it be embedded within the elements that I have not yet analyzed? Can I not see it because it is too soon for us to know how we will cease to inhabit this kingdom of man? Is this knowledge only for God to know and not for us to know?

Perhaps, the truth of the demise of humankind is there. Perhaps it is legible in the way humans have treated the Giza pyramid complex throughout the thousands of years it has existed- this amazing and generous gift from God. When humans made their way back to Giza after the Great Flood, some of them took the opportunity to use the existence of the complex to empower themselves. They created a government, a religion, and a culture that would honor one bloodline, and not God. Throughout the millennia, humans have credited the construction of the Giza pyramid complex to humans, instead of giving that credit to God. Humans devoted others' labor to trying to replicate the complex. Humans had themselves buried within the replica pyramids so that they could be memorialized after their deaths. When they were unable to replicate the size of the Great Pyramids successfully, their descendants claimed they had built the Great Pyramids and the lies were perpetuated to today. They even declared themselves to be Gods. How...Human!

And then, later humans, those who did not accept ancient Egyptian religion, desecrated the Complex through robbery and vandalism so that future generations could not have the details necessary to fully "read" it. All we are left with are questions and confusion. Humans may have created their own roadblock to gaining full understanding of the Truth about themselves. Not only did they eat from the Tree of Knowledge, they chopped it to pieces!

God said that He would never again create a Great

Flood to wipe Evil from the Earth. With Global Warming, I see that God doesn't have to do anything further to wipe Evil from Earth. I believe that God is going to leave that dirty deed to us. Perhaps Adam and Eve gave up what God had given them because they had no comparison to help them understand the potential consequences of making bad choices with their free will. We "modern" humans, on the other hand, have thousands of years of examples of good and bad choices available to us in the Bible. And yet, we have chosen behaviors that have led to the creation of tools with which we can destroy ourselves slowly, or very suddenly. God has described Heaven to us and instructed Jesus to list the ways to get there spiritually. Nonetheless, many of us continue to create Hell on Earth. Just as the solar analog range in which an alternate earthlike planet might exist is narrow, the path to Heaven is also narrow. In the Sermon on the Mount, as relayed in the book of Matthew, Jesus explained, in Matthew 7:13-14:

> Go in through the narrow gate, because broad is the gate and spacious is the road leading off into destruction, and many are going in through it; whereas narrow is the gate and cramped the road leading off into life, and few are finding it.

Humans lost access to eternal bodies, but had knowledge of good and evil. We know the difference and have communicated such knowledge throughout the ages through different media: from oral tradition to carving into stone, for standardization of information as it is passed from one generation to the next, and beyond. Humans have learned how to communicate knowledge beyond mortality by publishing on paper. Although digital records are easier to pass through long distances in an instant, they are ethereal and should not be depended on. In fact, paper deteriorates as well. So, the only way to guarantee preservation of knowledge is to put it in less pervious stone and present the knowledge symbolically. This is what I hypothesize God did with the Giza pyramid complex, and we are now capable of deciphering His Word, at least technologically.

With the help of ground penetrating technology, all of the precise details of the Giza pyramid complex soon will have been documented, and hopefully, graphically presented to the world. As of the publishing date of this book, many of the elements of the Giza pyramid complex have been documented using CAD (Computer Aided Design), by the University of Chicago; however, a complete rendering of its still to be discovered internal chambers have not. I believe that such information will provide all who are interested with the last remaining puzzle pieces they need to prove their hypotheses regarding who, when, and why the Giza pyramid complex was built. I am waiting excitedly for a complete rendering so that my hypothesis may be proven.

I have added my hypothesis regarding the Giza pyramid complex to numerous others with a primary purpose. I hope that my unique, mind-opening hypothesis will be dissected and analyzed by people of many disciplines who are also interested in the enigmatic puzzle created by the Giza pyramid complex. I am convinced that there is a link between the actual date of construction of the Giza pyramid complex and the creation of humans by God, according to the Bible. I believe that a collaborative, interdisciplinary analysis will be the key to unlock the solution to this ancient mystery. This book is an invitation to scientists and theologians of all disciplines to unite. Most of all, I have faith that the solution will reveal the path to world peace.

As in the conclusion of the ballad, "One Tin Soldier," by Dennis Lambert and Brian Potter: when the Valley People lifted the stone covering the treasure for which they had slaughtered all of the Mountain People, they discovered the words, "Peace on Earth".

APPENDIX A

Determining the x/y Proportion

As I explained in Chapter 7, in order to create a "ruler" for the Giza pyramid complex map, I used the workmen's barracks as a guide because they are so evenly divided. Unfortunately, when Petrie gave measurements of the workmen's barracks, he only gave the internal distance between the walls and not the overall length, which would include the walls of the barracks. Fortunately, Petrie, having been a surveyor, left accurate drawings of the barracks. One drawing Petrie included in the original edition of *The Pyramids and Temples of Gizeh*, contained a scale drawing of the workmen's barracks and the Khafre Pyramid. (This drawing was excluded in the edition rewritten by Hawass.) I was able to count the number of each group of barracks; however, because Petrie did not give a measurement for the total length of either group of barracks (so that I could determine the distance between the centers of the walls), I needed to find other elements within the Giza pyramid complex of equal length and for which measurements had been given.

Using a ruler, I found that the length of the north to south barracks was equal to the diagonal of the base of the Khufu Pyramid. Fortunately, because Lehner gave accurate measurements of the base of the Khufu Pyramid in his book, *The Complete Pyramids*, I could use trigonometry to find the length of the diagonal of its base (325.74m) and apply that length to the length of the north to south barracks, as you can see on Plate 7-6. When I divided 325.74m by 73 barracks, I was able to determine that the average width of each barrack is 4.46m. This is the length I used for one Giza y, or g(y), unit.

As a comparison for the length of the east to west barracks, I found that the north and south walls of the base of the Menkaure Pyramid were of equivalent length. (Lehner gave different dimensions for two of the four base walls than for the other two; hence the determination that the base of the Menkaure Pyramid is rectangular. However, Lehner did not designate which pair

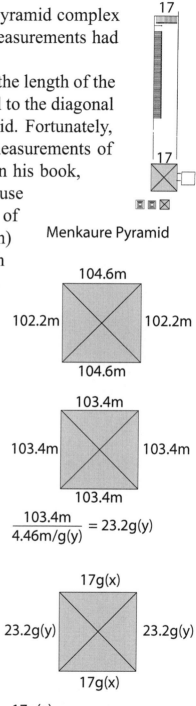

Menkaure Pyramid

$$\frac{103.4m}{4.46m/g(y)} = 23.2g(y)$$

$$\frac{17g(x)}{23.2g(y)} = 0.733 \; g(x)/g(y)$$

of walls is longer, so I used the average of the two lengths (103.4m) as the equivalent to the length of the east to west barracks.) Because one g(y) unit equals 4.46m, 103.4m divided by 4.46m equals 23.2 g(y) units. This represents the number of g(y) units on the x-axis represented by the east to west barracks.

I explained in Chapter 6 (see Plate 6-3) that there are a total of 17 east to west barracks. This is the number of g(x) units on the x-axis. Therefore, the ratio of g(x) units to g(y) units on the x-axis is equal to 17 g(x) divided by 23.2 g(y), or 0.733 g(x)/g(y). Hence, the ratio of x/y is 0.733:1 and the ratio of y/x is 1.36:1.

THE SPHINX.

Ancient Egypt, its Monuments and History , 1851
D. P. Kidder

APPENDIX B

Determining the Giza z Unit

It has long been known that the Khufu Pyramid has a unique geometric and mathematical design (Plate B-1). If the perimeter of the base of the Khufu Pyramid (which measures 921.32m) is converted to the circular base of

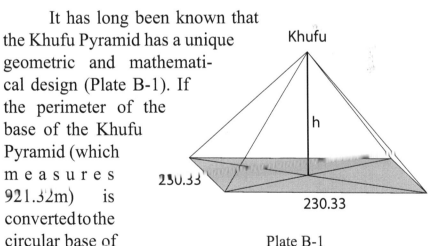

Plate B-1

a cone (having the same circumference of 921.32m); and if the height of the cone is the same as the height of the Khufu Pyramid, the radius of the cone would be equal to its height (Plate B-2). This conical conversion is only perfectly applicable to the Khufu Pyramid which, I believe, makes this

Khufu Pyramid Adjusted to Cone

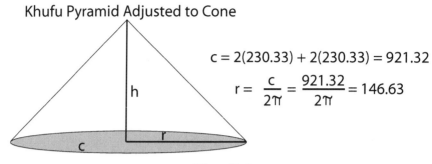

$$c = 2(230.33) + 2(230.33) = 921.32$$

$$r = \frac{c}{2\pi} = \frac{921.32}{2\pi} = 146.63$$

Plate B-2

property significant.

The casing stones of the apex of the Khafre Pyramid, as well as its base stones, are preserved to this day (possibly because the base stones were made of unpolished granite, and hence, not desirable for repurposing). Hence, accurate measurements are still able to be made. If one applies the conical conversion to the base perimeter and height of the Khafre Pyramid, the radius of the resulting cone does not equal the height of the cone.

Menkaure Pyramid

Over time, the Menkaure Pyramid has deteriorated and its height cannot be measured accurately.

102.2

h

104.6

Plate B-3

rately. Mark Lehner, in his book, *The Complete Pyramids*, provides a measurement of, "about 65 meters" for its height. He also provides an angle to which the Menkaure Pyramid rises to its apex, which I used in Chapter 7. It occurred to me that, since the Menkaure Pyramid has a rectangular base and not a square base, if the pyramid's apex is a point, there should be two angles of rise (Plate B-3). However, when I

Menkaure Pyramid Adjusted to Cone

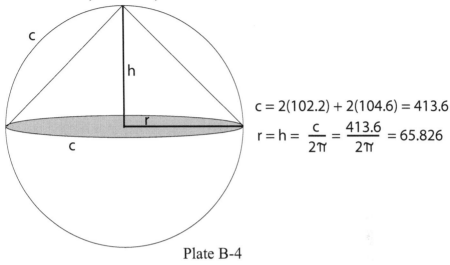

$$c = 2(102.2) + 2(104.6) = 413.6$$

$$r = h = \frac{c}{2\pi} = \frac{413.6}{2\pi} = 65.826$$

Plate B-4

performed the conical conversion to the Menkaure Pyramid, as performed on the Khufu Pyramid, I found that the radius calculates to 65.826m (Plate B-4). This value is close to the "about 65 meters" value for the height, as provided by Mark

Menkaure Pyramid Adjusted to Square Base

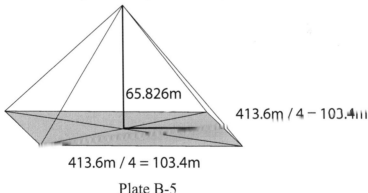

65.826m

413.6m / 4 – 103.4m

413.6m / 4 = 103.4m

Plate B-5

Lehner in his book, *The Complete Pyramids*. Hence, I used the more precise measurement of 65.826m as the height of the Menkaure Pyramid in my calculations (Plate B-5).

Out of curiosity, I squared the base of the Menkaure

Pyramid by adding the width to the length and dividing by two. This resulted in a base measurement of 103.4m x 103.4m. Then, I substituted the calculated height of 65.826m and recalculated the angle at which the pyramid rises to its apex. The new angle calculated to 51 degrees, 51 minutes, 19.66 seconds and this is the angle I used to perform comparisons with the other pyramids.

While evaluating the Khufu and Menkaure Pyramids with respect to the radius-to-height equivalence present in these converted structures, it occurred to me that this relationship might be significant when building a three-dimensional, Cartesian model. In order to describe a point in a three-dimensional space, a "z" value must be included with the "x" and "y" values.

[Cartesian coordinates (x,y,z) are used to describe points in space. This system is used to build a model that can be converted to spherical coordinates, which are used in Astronomy to describe an angle from a reference direction on a plane, and an angle over (or under) the plane to the object, which provides a direction. The distance to the object provides the location, represented in spherical coordinate format, of a point in space.]

In a spherical coordinate system, the angular measure has a relationship to the actual distance between points, called their "angular separation". When considering a change in latitude (y value), the angular separation, from one latitude to the next, remains constant. This angle is also representative of a distance (Plate B-6).

A characteristic of longitude (x value) is that the angular separation, from one longitude to the next, represents a different distance, depending on the position of latitudes with respect to the "equator" of the sphere. In this case, the "equator" of our spherical coordinate system is the ecliptic

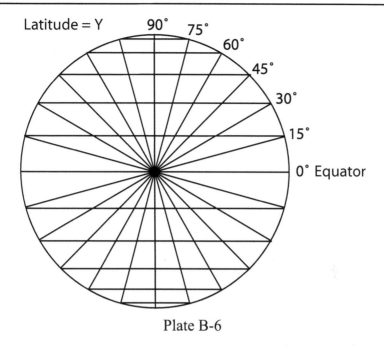

Plate B-6

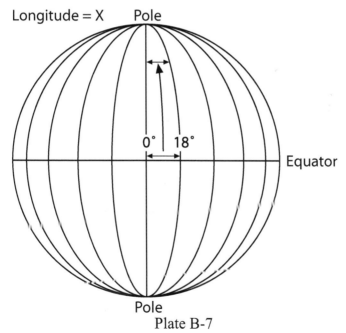

Pole
Plate B-7

plane (Plate B-7).

Using the special property of the conical conversion

of the Khufu Pyramid, the height equals the radius. Applying this property to a spherical coordinate system:

$$z \text{ (height)} = y \text{ (radius)}$$

Or:

$$\text{Altitude} = \text{Latitude}$$

I used latitude, instead of longitude for two reasons: as stated in the last paragraph, the angular separation from any latitude to the next does not change; and because the angle represented at any given latitude also represents a distance in a spherical coordinate system. This is why we chose the y value to be equivalent to the z value.

Bibliography

New World Translation of the Holy Scriptures, New York, 2013

Possibility Thinkers Bible, New York, 1984

Aldred, Cyril — *Egypt to the end of the Old Kingdom*, London, 1965

Degani, Meir H. — *Astronomy Made Simple*, New York, 1976

Fagan, Brian — *Egypt of the Pharaohs*, Washington D.C., 2001

Harper Collins — *Past Worlds Atlas of Archaeology*, London, 1997

Hawass, Zahi — 136 page re-write of W.M.F. Petrie's 315 page; *The Pyramids and Temples of Gizeh,* London, 1990

James, T.G.H. — *The Archaeology of Ancient Egypt*, London, 1972

Kerrod, Robin — *The Star Guide Learning How to Read the Night Sky Star By Star,* New York, 1993

Kidder, D.P. — *Ancient Egypt, Its Monuments and History, 1851*

La Riche, William — *Alexandria the Sunken City*, London, 1996

Lehner, Mark — *The Complete Pyramids*, London, 1997

Macaulay, David — *Pyramid*, Boston, 1975

Marincola, John — *Herodotus The Histories*, New York, 1996

Mercer, Samuel A.B. — *The Pyramid Texts*, New York, 1952

Mosley, John — *Starry Night Companion*, Toronto, 2003

Palmer, Claude Irwin & Leigh, Charles Wilber — *Plane und Spherical Trigonometry*, London, 1934

Petrie, W.M.F. — *A History of Egypt Vol. 1*, London, 1897

Petrie, W.M.F. — *Ten Years' Digging in Egypt, 1881-1891*, London, 1892

Petrie, W.M.F.   *The Pyramids and Temples of Gizeh*, London, 1883

Richardson, Dan &   *The Rough Guide to Egypt*, London, 2010
Jacobs, Daniel

Rossi, Corinna   *The Pyramids and the Sphinx*, Italy, 2005

Shaw, Ian, Oxford   *Ancient Egypt*, New York, 2000
University Press

Siliotti, Alberto   *Guide to the Valley of the Kings*, Italy, 1996

Smyth, Piazzi   *Life and Work at the Great Pyramid*, Vol 1,
                      Scotland, 1867

Smyth, Piazzi   *Life and Work at the Great Pyramid*, Vol 2,
                      Scotland, 1867

Smyth, Piazzi   *Our inheritance in the Great Pyramid*, London,
                      1874

Tompkins, Peter   *Secrets of the Great Pyramid*, New York, 1971

Vyse, Howard-R.   *Operations carried on at the pyramids of
                      Gizeh in 1837 Vol. 1 & 2,* London, 1840

Web Resources

BBC News Online   Great Pyramid: Lost Egyptian artefact found in
                      Aberdeen cigar box,
                      BBC Internet, December 16, 2020, bbc.com/news/
                      uk-scotland-north-east-orkney-shetland-55315623

University of Chicago Giza Plateau Computer Model
Oriental Institute   oi.uchicago.edu/research/projects/giza-plateau-
                      computer-model

Wikipedia   Charles Taze Russell
                      Wikipedia Internet, en.wikipedia.org/wiki/Charles_
                      Taze_Russell

Made in the USA
Columbia, SC
12 March 2023

13668581R00074